GEORGE B

EIGHT MONTHS' CAMPAIGN

AGAINST THE

BENGAL SEPOY ARMY

DURING THE MUTINY OF 1857

Elibron Classics
www.elibron.com

Elibron Classics series.

© 2005 Adamant Media Corporation.

ISBN 1-4021-8752-1 (paperback)
ISBN 1-4212-9580-6 (hardcover)

This Elibron Classics Replica Edition is an unabridged facsimile
of the edition published in 1858 by Smith, Elder & Co.,
London.

EIGHT MONTHS' CAMPAIGN

AGAINST THE

BENGAL SEPOY ARMY,

DURING THE MUTINY OF 1857.

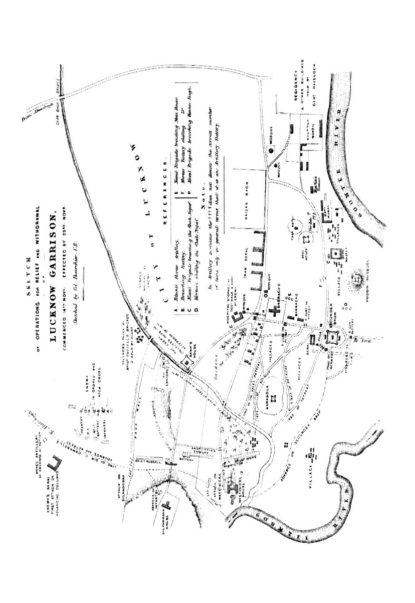

SKETCH
OF OPERATIONS FOR RELIEF AND WITHDRAWAL
OF
LUCKNOW GARRISON,
COMMENCED 14TH NOVR. EFFECTED BY 23RD NOVR.

Sketched by Col. Baird-Smith C.B.

CITY OF LUCKNOW

REFERENCES.

A. Shanks Horse Artillery.
B. Breaching Battery.
C. Naval Brigade breaching the Shah Nujeef.
D. Mortars shelling the Shah Nujeef.
E. Naval Brigade breaching Mess House.
F. Mortar Battery shelling Do.
P. Naval Brigade breaching Banner Bungh.

Note.

In artillery positions the †††† does not denote the correct number of Guns but only in general terms that it is an Artillery Battery.

GOOMTEE RIVER

GOOMTEE RIVER

EIGHT MONTHS' CAMPAIGN

AGAINST THE

BENGAL SEPOY ARMY,

DURING THE MUTINY OF 1857.

BY

COLONEL GEORGE BOURCHIER, C.B.,

BENGAL HORSE ARTILLERY,
LATE COMMANDING NO. 17 LIGHT FIELD BATTERY.

THE MASSACRE HOUSE, CAWNPORE.

LONDON:
SMITH, ELDER AND CO., 65, CORNHILL.

1858.

TO

AN AGED MOTHER.

WHOSE LIFE HAS BEEN ONE LONG EFFORT TO PROMOTE

THE HAPPINESS OF HER FAMILY,

This Narrative

IS DEDICATED WITH EVERY FEELING OF ATTACHMENT,

BY A DUTIFUL AND AFFECTIONATE

SON.

Lahore, 21st March, 1858.

PREFACE.

For all defects in the following pages, which originally were intended for private circulation, the author has but one apology, that the notes from which it has been compiled were taken just as opportunities could be snatched from more important duties. The details of the "Siege of Delhi" have been taken from Major Norman's journal; much other information has been gleaned therefrom, and from the public despatches.

The account of the mutiny at Cawnpore was given to me by Mr. Sherer, Civil Service, at that station: its author I do not know.

LIST OF ILLUSTRATIONS.

CONTENTS.

CHAPTER I.

CHAPTER V.

CHAPTER VI.

CHAPTER VII.

CHAPTER VIII.

CHAPTER XII.

CONCLUDING CHAPTER.

NARRATIVE

OF

EIGHT MONTHS' CAMPAIGN

AGAINST THE

SEPOY ARMY OF BENGAL.

CHAPTER I.

OUTBREAK OF THE MUTINY.

POLITICIANS at various times had prophesied that we should some morning awake and find that our Indian Empire had melted from our grasp. The enormous increase to the native army by the contingents raised to guard the newly acquired territories of Gwalior, the Punjaub, and Oude, with no corresponding increase to the European force, gave the native population reason to think that they had every chance of being able to drive our small European force from the country. From circumstances which have since come to light, it is clear that a simultaneous rising was intended on some Sunday, while all the

[8]   B

European troops were at church; the conduct of the native troops at Meerut precipitated matters, and prevented such a terrible consummation, which, utterly unprepared as was the country, could not have been withstood.

Many reasons have been assigned for the rising; but, to use the words of the late lamented General Nicholson, than whom none more fully understood the native character, "Neither greased cartridges, the annexation of Oude, nor the paucity of European officers were the causes. For years," he said, "I have watched the army, and felt sure they only wanted their opportunity to try their strength with us."

Whatever may have been the causes, in the commencement of 1857 the first deep mutterings of the storm were heard: at Barrackpore and Berhampore, a strong mutinous spirit was displayed. Whether more stringent measures might not have crushed the mutiny at its outset, is a point now past arguing upon. Few were willing to believe that the tornado was more than a transient cloud. More than one regiment at Barrackpore was disbanded; the General and his mutinous sepoys parted, shedding "idle tears;" the former to return to temporise with those who as yet were not in open mutiny, the latter to join their brethren at Delhi, where arms by thousands were ready to their hands.

On the 13th of May the news of the mutiny and massacre at Meerut reached Sealkote.

The troops at Mean Meer by timely energy were disarmed; but still Brigadier Brind, who commanded at Sealkote, would not believe that the infection had spread to the regiments under his command. The artillery, with that fatal security which had lulled all India into the most stolid incredulity of the hurricane about to burst, was isolated from the only European regiment at the station.

To remedy this, my battery was ordered up to the lines of H. M.'s 52nd, while a portion of that regiment was sent for the protection of Colonel Dawes' troop of Horse Artillery; thus bringing the two Native Infantry corps between the fires of both batteries, and cutting off their communication with the 9th Light Cavalry, which was on the left, thrown back. The arrangement was a most judicious one.

The season in which the mutiny broke out formed one of its most terrible features. Though the mutterings were heard early in the year, no active measures were taken until after the Meerut massacre in May; at which time, on ordinary occasions, all European soldiers are prohibited from leaving their barracks from 8 A. M. until near sunset, and unnecessary exposure under canvas would be considered madness. The emergency required that not only should the army take the field, but that the ladies and children should be sent to some place of safety.

Sir John Lawrence recommended that all from Sealkote should be sent to Lahore.

The wives and children of the soldiers were *ordered* over under escort; but few ladies attended to the advice so wisely tendered, and those who remained reaped the horrors of the mutiny of the 9th July.

A Punjabee of wealth and high reputation, to whom I had been of some service, volunteered, if I would place my wife and two children under his charge, to escort them to Lahore; after the massacres at Delhi and Meerut it was a terribly anxious undertaking, but I resolved implicitly to trust him, and nobly he fulfilled his promise.

To add to our troubles, the two children were suffering, the one from cramp the other from ophthalmia; but Providence, whose protecting hand had been so marked in our favour during this eventful year, brought them safely through their journey to Lahore, where the open doors and warm hearts of my friends Mr. and Mrs. Montgomery, were open to receive them.

For the army at large, who were turned into camp at this inclement season, little could be done; tents with the thermometer at 120 cannot be pleasant under any circumstances.

"A jolly growl was all the art I knew,
To make me happy and to keep me so."

But I anticipate events. it was on the 20th of May that orders were received for the formation of a moveable column to patrol the Punjaub, for the suppression of the mutiny. To raise the required force it was necessary to withdraw the European troops from Sealkote. Sir John Lawrence implored Brigadier Brind not to fancy that the political horizon was growing clearer; adding that the interests of individual stations must not be allowed to interfere with the salvation of the country. Yet even with this warning, and the fact that it had been found necessary to disarm the troops at Mean Meer, the 46th Native Infantry and a wing of the 9th Cavalry remained armed at Sealkote until after the withdrawal of the European troops; when to disarm them was impossible.

This infatuation was not singular: nothing in the history of the revolution seems more wonderful than the temper evinced by every officer of the native army, if you only hinted at the probability of *his* corps going wrong; while the same man would willingly allow that no other was safe: the truth of the old proverb, that "every crow thinks its own bairn the whitest," was fully evinced; but gradually every bairn showed, as he slipped away from the parent hand, that he was not a bit better than his neighbours.

On the night of the 25th of May, the Sealkote Brigade,* consisting of H. M.'s 52nd, Colonel Dawes' Troop of Horse Artillery, No. 17 Battery, a wing of the 9th Cavalry, and the 35th Light Infantry, marched, and on the morning of the 27th joined the remainder of the column at Wuzeerabad.

Many alterations had been made in its original organization, consequent on the threatening aspect of affairs in the north of the Punjaub; but even then that noble policy of denuding the Punjaub to rescue the North-Western Provinces (and which may be said to have been the salvation of India) was in progress. Regiments of Punjaubees were being pushed rapidly towards Delhi by marches which appeared fabulous; new levies were rising as if

---

* Two hundred of H. M.'s 52nd, with two guns of Colonel Dawes' Troop, remained for some days behind the column, but subsequently joined it. The regiment originally ordered was the 46th N. I.; but Brigadier Brind fancied the 46th was more trustworthy, and he therefore obtained permission to retain it and send on the 35th N. I.

by magic; and all departments evinced the energy of the master-mind which guided the operations of the Punjaub.

Having organized his column at Wuzeerabad, Brigadier-General Chamberlain, who had been appointed to command, marched on the morning of the 28th for Lahore, arriving on the banks of the Ravee at Shadarah on the 1st of June.

It was thought not improbable that the native troops might show some disinclination to cross the bridge; secret instructions were given to meet this emergency, and, although it did not become necessary to carry them out, they showed that General Chamberlain had no idea of half measures, should coercion have been required.

On the 29th, at Goojranwalla, the Rev. Cave Brown, our appointed chaplain, had joined the camp and shared my tent.* The column remained some days at Lahore.

On the 9th of June, at Anarkullee, two sepoys of the 35th were tried by a drum-head court-martial for mutinous language, and sentenced to be blown

---

* It may be well to explain to the uninitiated that when in camp in hot weather, the most effective plan is to pile the bedclothes on your bed to check the direct influence of the rays of the sun, and lie yourself underneath it. In this predicament Mr. Cave Brown found me, and willingly took possession of the upper storey.

away from the guns. The execution was a terrible one. Having been directed to carry it out in my battery, I was close to the wretches, and could watch every feature; they showed the most perfect apathy: one man merely saying that he had some money in the hands of the non-commissioned officer of his company; the other never uttered a word.[*]

This was the first tragedy of the kind carried out, and must have struck awe and terror into the minds of all who witnessed it.

Deeming it expedient that the presence of a large body of European troops should be known throughout the Punjaub, on the 10th of June General Chamberlain marched the column to Umritsur, arriving on the morning of the 11th. On the evening of that day a fakeer, who had been caught tampering with some of Colonel Coke's regiment of Punjaubees, was hung not only in front of the force assembled, but in the presence of nearly the whole population of Umritsur, who crowded out to witness the execution.

The weather continued very oppressive, but the

---

[*] Since this execution I have seen many men hung and executed in various ways. They all evinced the same indifference as to life or death; one man bowed his head to me as he was being tied to the gun and said, "Salaam, Captain Sahib, Salaam, gora log," "Good-bye Captain, good-bye Europeans."

European troops were accommodated in the palace in the Ram Bagh in comparative comfort.

On the 14th of June the force again marched towards the Jullundur Dooab, crossing the river Beeas on the 18th, and arriving at Jullundur on the 20th.

While at Umritsur the news was received of the engagements at Badul-ka-Serai, the death of the Adjutant-General of the army, Colonel Chester, and the appointment of General Chamberlain to fill this vacant position. Colonel Nicholson, an officer also well known in the Punjaub, took command of the column on the 22nd, and on the 24th left Jullundur for Phillore. No sooner had General Nicholson joined the column than he made his presence felt among us; an expeditionary force was organized for any sudden and lengthened enterprise, in which our foot infantry could not possibly have kept up.

His arrangements were to keep three of the Horse Artillery guns intact, to mount the remainder of the troop as cavalry, while twelve ammunition waggons, emptied, were to carry provisions for a certain number of days; and on each waggon nine riflemen of H. M.'s 52nd were mounted as a guard for the guns, or for any offensive operations.

Although the force was never brought into action,

the arrangement for the purpose required would have been found most useful and effective.

Within four miles of Jullundur the road from Hooshiarpore joins the trunk road. At the latter station was cantoned the 33rd Native Infantry, to whom orders were despatched to join the column at Phillore by a forced march.

General Nicholson knew full well that, although not in open mutiny, to leave this regiment armed in his rear was fraught with danger; while already with his own column he had a force of native infantry and cavalry exceeding in numbers his Europeans: to use his own words, "Mutiny is like small-pox, it spreads quickly, and must be crushed as soon as possible."

On the morning of the 25th of June the column marched under the walls of the Fort of Phillore. The artillery, with H. M.'s 52nd on either flank, were drawn up on the right of the road unlimbered. The 35th, little dreaming of the trap into which they were led, marched unconsciously up the road in column, and not until within a short distance of the guns did the true light of their position dawn upon them; quietly they piled their arms, which were taken to the fort. The 33rd followed their example, and were dealt with in a similar manner.

No doubt can exist as to the wisdom of this measure; reports were current, and authentic information had been, I believe, received that the 35th were in communication with the mutineers at Delhi, and only waited their opportunity, with the wing of the 9th Cavalry, to attack the column; the only reason the latter was not disarmed was the effect it might have had on the other wing at Sealkote.

The manner in which the disarming was carried out showed the greatest tact on the part of the Commander; orders had been sent to the police at the bridge of boats that, at the first sound of firing, the bridge was to be cut away.

Well do I remember, as leaning over one of my guns, the coolness with which he gave every order; his last was, " If they bolt, you follow as hard as you can, the bridge will have been destroyed, and we shall have a second Sobraon on a small scale." As the regiments marched from the ground on which they had been disarmed, General Nicholson warned them that any attempt at desertion should be punished by death, that the fords were watched, and that it was impossible to escape. Eight tried their luck; all were caught and were executed, after trial by drum-head courts-martial.

CHAPTER II.

PURSUIT OF THE MUTINEERS.

So far the immediate object of the march of the column to Phillore had been accomplished; but still the state of the Punjaub was matter of anxiety: at Rawul Pindee, Jhelum, Sealkote, and Kote Kangra, were stationed native corps, still armed; it was therefore advisable that the column should return to Umritsur, where it would be in a more central position to act on any point required.

Leaving Phillore on the 28th, we again crossed the Beeas, not as formerly by a bridge of boats; the river had risen, the bridge was carried away, and it was necessary to embark guns, horses, &c., on board boats. As General Nicholson bade adieu to the political commissioner, Captain Farrington, on the bank, I heard him say, " You 'll soon see me back again:" his words were prophetic, as will hereafter appear.

We arrived at Umritsur on the 5th of July, without any striking incident save the execution of a few deserters.

On our arrival we found that reports were current that the regiment at Jhelum (the 14th N. I.) had mutinied. This rumour was confirmed, with the addition, that on the 9th of July the 46th, a wing of the 9th Cavalry, had also mutinied at Sealkote, and murdered all the officers they could catch hold of; that Brigadier Brind, Captain Bishop, the two Doctors Graham, and the Rev. Mr. Hunter, his wife and child, were the victims; moreqver, that the mutinous troops were in full march on Goordaspore, to be joined by Jackson's Irregular Cavalry Corps and the regiment from Kote Kangra.

The 33rd Native Infantry had been left disarmed at Jullundur. The 35th were encamped half-way between Umritsur and the banks of the Beeas, so that little anxiety existed on their account.

The 59th and wing of the 9th Cavalry were immediately disarmed, and the European portion of the column, consisting of nine guns, H. M.'s 52nd, some companies of Punjaub Infantry, and some newly raised cavalry levies, were prepared for a forced march to intercept the Sealkote Brigade of mutineers.

On the evening of the 10th of July, at 9 P. M., we started, and on the following morning, arrived at Battala, twenty-six miles on the road to Goordaspore; where we were informed that it was intended to push on direct to the latter station, still eighteen miles distant.

A halt was called for a couple of hours; bread and rum with an abundance of milk was served out. All were aware what a terrific sunning we might expect; none knew it better than Nicholson, but he knew also the value of the stake.

It was in a difficulty of this kind, that his valuable qualities shone forth in grasping the resources of the country. 200 pony carriages (ekhas) with all the ponies belonging to the grass-cutters of the 9th Cavalry, carried as many as possible of the 52nd; while the Cavalry horses were made over to the Sikhs.*

With these appliances even, many fell victims to the heat. When mounted, it was bad enough, but for an infantry soldier, with his musket and sixty rounds of ammunition in pouch, it was terrific.

Yet under these circumstances, trying as they were, the spirit of fun was not extinct; the artillery made extemporary awnings of branches of trees over their gun-carriages and waggons, giving them the appearance of carts "got up" for a day at Hampstead; officers crowned with wreaths of green leaves, were "chaffed" by their comrades for adopting head-dresses

* Every Sikh or Punjaubee can ride.

à la Norma. Here might be seen a soldier on a
rampant pony, desiring his companion on a similar
beast, " to keep behind and be his ' edge de camp,' "
there a hero, mindful perhaps of Epping on Easter
Monday, bellowing out his inquiries as to " who had
seen the fox?" Privates never intended for the
mounted branch, here and there came to grief and
lay sprawling on mother-earth, while ever and
anon some mighty Jehu in his ekha dashed to the
front at a pace a Roman charioteer would have
envied.

All things must have an end. The Artillery
arrived at Goordaspore at 3 P. M. on the 11th, having
been eighteen hours on the road; the infantry did
not arrive until three hours later.

Three artillery horses were shot, and all were much
knocked up; but the district was saved. The mutineers were only eight miles distant on the banks
of the Ravee, never dreaming but that the column
was still at Umritsur.

Longer marches have been made, but none severer,
or attended with more satisfactory results. Number-
less were the reports which were spread during the
evening and the following morning, as to the operations of the enemy. So carefully was the road to the
river guarded, that not a hint had they received as

to the whereabouts of the column; neither had the
views of General Nicholson got wind in camp.

Early on the morning of the 12th we were ordered
to change our ground; and bitter was the disappointment in the belief that the enemy had
slipped through our fingers, or having received
some intimation of our advent, had retreated into
the hills.

It was premature: at what was eventually to be
our encamping ground, near H. M.'s 52nd, we
halted, and were soon joined by the remainder of the
force.

It soon spread far and wide, that the enemy had
crossed the Ravee river with all their baggage;
and though certain of another day's grilling, we had
the excitement of feeling that the mutinous scoundrels
who had so recently shed the blood of our friends at
Sealkote, were within our grasp.

The 52nd, still wearied with their terrific march
of the previous day, pressed on as if fatigue was
unknown to them. At about 1 P.M., we came in
sight of the advanced videttes of the 9th Cavalry,
dancing about in their grey jackets. General Nicholson thinking only of getting " a good bag "—in fact
hoping that, with the river in their rear, he would
be able to annihilate the enemy—masked his column

by a line of Punjaub-mounted Police,* and marched
to within musket range of their line before a shot
was fired.

I confess that I felt nervous as to the conduct
of my native drivers; although not a shadow of
suspicion attached to them, yet who could say at
what moment they might not turn against us? The
trial was in this case a most severe one; they were
being led against men with whom they had been for
years associated at Sealkote. I took the precaution
to warn my European gunners to watch them. In
the reply of my Farrier-Sergeant spoke the whole
company, "If they only attempt to run, sir, we'll
cut all their heads off." But in this case, as in every
other, my native drivers nobly did their duty; and
although the senior non-commissioned officer was a
man of the lowest caste, a more gallant soldier never
lived: he led my No. 1 gun through every action,
and has met his reward by being promoted to the
highest commissioned grade of subadar, by Sir Colin
Campbell.

But to return to the engagement of Trimmoo
Ghât. The ground chosen by the enemy was most

---

* These were levies only just raised, badly armed and undis-
ciplined, but who subsequently performed such good service as
"Hodson's Horse."

favourable for their operations; in their front was a
deep narrow strip of water, over which was only
one bridge, and their flanks were protected by
villages. Scarcely had the Artillery crossed the
bridge, and were forming on the opposite side,
screened by the Punjaub levies, than down came the
9th Cavalry on their flanks (before the 52nd could
form to receive them) gnashing their teeth, and
worked up to the utmost with intoxicating drugs:
they cut right and left at the gunners and drivers.
Away scampered the mounted levies back to Goordaspore; the enemy pushed out their skirmishers to
within fifty yards of the guns, and a tremendous
volley from the whole line, delivered as simul-
taneously as if on parade at Sealkote, made things
at first look very ugly.

In five minutes the scene was changed: not a
trooper of the 9th Cavalry who charged the guns
left the batteries alive. The infantry formed on our
flanks, and a well-directed pounding of grape and
shrapnell, from nine guns, aided by the rifles of the
infantry, soon told its tale. In about twenty minutes
the fire of the enemy was subdued; in ten minutes
more they were in full retreat towards the river,
leaving between three or four hundred killed and
wounded on the field.

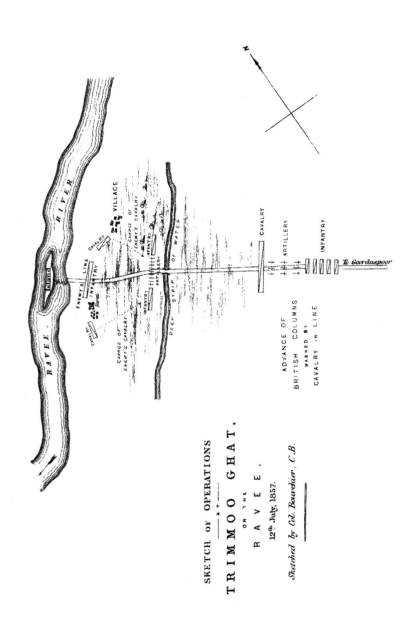

SKETCH of OPERATIONS
— AT —
TRIMMOO GHAT,
ON THE
RAVEE.
12th July, 1857.

Sketched by Col. Bourchier, C.B.

Had the General but possessed a squadron or two of Cavalry, not a man could have escaped. The Sikhs, less done up by the sun than the Europeans, advanced, gallantly led by Lieutenant Boswell. The horses were nearly as much done up as the men, and could hardly get up a canter to the river bank; where we took possession of all the baggage and stores crossed over by the enemy, consisting chiefly of arms, ammunition, and clothing, the property of Government; and carriages, furniture, and property belonging to the officers at Sealkote.

At the river we immediately came under the fire of an iron gun, which, with immense labour, they had dragged with them, and posted on an island, 1,100 yards from the main bank. To attempt to cross that evening was impossible; a few rounds were fired at a party of men standing round the gun, which dispersed them into the jungle.

Leaving the Punjaub Infantry, under Lieutenant Boswell, to keep the Ford and protect the captured property, the column returned that evening to Goordaspore. Thus ended the first day's operations against the Sealkote Brigade.

It was long after dark before we arrived in camp, I can fairly say, dead beat. A sergeant died by my side of sheer exhaustion, and many of the 52nd shared the same fate. None who have not experienced it know what those exposed on a battle-field suffer in India in the month of July. As we were returning to camp, my servant brought me a bottle of beer; I poured out a tumbler; a sergeant of the 52nd passed me, and fairly turned round to stare at it: such a look of exhaustion I never before saw; he said not a word. I offered him the tumbler; his " God bless you, sir!" was an ample reward.

Although the rebels on the opposite bank had been well thrashed, they seemed in no way inclined to give up their property and position without another brush for it; in fact, they knew not where to go to: foiled by General Nicholson's masterly move on Goordaspore, and shrewdly guessing that the column which had defeated the Jhelum Brigade was in their rear, to stand and fight was their dernier resort. Some attempted to recross from the island to the main land; those who escaped drowning either fell into the hands of the police, or, trying their luck in Cashmere, were delivered over to our Government by the Maharajah, Golab Sing.

Various reports were sent up during the day from the river as to their tactics; and at one time it was believed that, imagining our retiring to our camp at

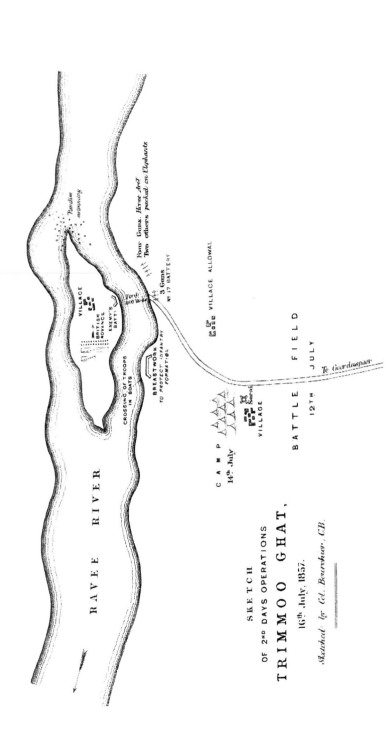

RAVEE RIVER

VILLAGE

BRITISH ADVANCE

ENEMY'S BATTY

Parhāes

Banning

Four Guns. Horse Arty
Two others packed on Elephants

Ford 1000 Yards

3 Guns
Nº 17 BATTERY

VILLAGE ALLOWAL

CROSSING OF TROOPS IN BOATS

BREASTWORK
TO PROTECT INFANTRY FORMAT: ON

CAMP
14ᵗʰ July

Serai
VILLAGE

BATTLE FIELD
12ᵗʰ JULY

To Goordaspoor

SKETCH
OF 2ᴺᴰ DAYS OPERATIONS
TRIMMOO GHAT,
16ᵗʰ July, 1857.
Sketched by Ct. Bourchier, CB.

Goordaspore was a sign of weakness, the mutineers were again attempting to cross.

In the afternoon of the 14th the column marched to the banks of the river, and there encamped, just out of reach of the battery on the island. Some delay was caused by the great difficulty in procuring boats.

On the morning of the 16th, however, they were prepared; two of Colonel Dawes' Horse Artillery guns were mounted on elephants, ready to be crossed, if required, by the ford. My battery was placed in the open, to draw off Pandy's attention from the real game.

At daylight the ball commenced. The scheme succeeded admirably; half the 52nd were across, and had formed before the enemy were aware that a boat even had been procured. At last the true state of things glimmered on their understandings, "their stronghold was invaded." Troopers galloped about, the assembly was sounded over and over again, and the gun was slewed round to arrest the progress of the line; to silence it at such a distance (1,200 yards) while it was nearly concealed by grass and an earthen breastwork, was all but impossible. Covered by the fire of our seven guns, the line advanced, headed by General Nicholson, a powerful swordsman.

It was a beautiful sight. Nothing could have been managed in a more orderly manner. The gun, fortunately, had been so much elevated to throw across the river, that now it carried harmlessly over the advancing line.*

The battery, and subsequently the village in and around which their camp was pitched, were taken and destroyed. A miscellaneous mob of sepoys, villagers, and camp followers, fled to the end of the island, where those who escaped the bayonet took to the river. The few who succeeded in gaining the opposite shore received no mercy from the villagers, who drove them back into the water.

The chastisement thus inflicted was signal; if not utterly destroyed, the mutinous brigade was disorganised, and all danger of any mischief, as far as they were concerned, at an end. The column returned to Umritsur on the 22nd to await fresh operations.

* The gun was one used to fire the morning and evening gun at Sealkote; its elevating screw was an old Sikh affair and not easily worked.

CHAPTER III.

A FLYING VISIT TO SIMLAH.

LITTLE did we dream on the morning of the 22nd of July, when our tents were pitched at Umritsur, that before many hours we should receive orders to fill up our ammunition and march the following morning towards the Beeas.

General Nicholson had left the column prior to its arrival at Umritsur, to attend the chief commissioner, Sir J. Lawrence, at Lahore; thence flashed the order of march. Rumours of all kinds were, as usual, abroad as to our destination; few believed it possible that we could be destined for Delhi: the danger of leaving the Punjaub with such a handful of European troops rendered such a step improbable; but the self-sacrificing policy which had already so far denuded that province of troops was to be stretched still further. General Nicholson's last words to the political agent, when parting with him on the Beeas, seemed prophetic, "You 'll soon see me back again."

Nothing for certain was known until the 24th,
when General Nicholson joined the camp at Reeah;
all speculations were then at an end: "we were to
join the army before Delhi;" our only fears were
that it would fall before we possibly could arrive
there.

One thing all felt certain of, that it would not be
the fault of our commanding officer if we did not
arrive in time.

On the 25th of July we again crossed the Beeas
and commenced a series of forced marches towards
the Sutlej.

I must now digress, from the progress of the
column, to scenes of a domestic character.

As long as it was intended that the column should
merely patrol the Punjaub, I felt that Lahore was
the best place for my family. Independently of the
great kindness of my friends, who cared for them
and protected them during this period of intense
anxiety, I had occasionally hopes of a run into
Lahore; but now that the column was to leave the
Punjaub, it was necessary to choose a fixed place
of residence for them. Simlah, in the Himalayas,
offered the advantages of quiet with a splendid
climate and fine scenery. General Nicholson, always
ready to be kind to his officers, granted me leave

of absence, on the understanding that I rejoined prior to marching into Delhi.

On the 27th of July I mounted the mail cart; on the 28th made all preparations for leaving Lahore, and on the 29th, at 2 P.M., started from Mr. and Mrs. Montgomery's house for Simlah, feeling deeply grateful for all their kindness.

Having only at the most a fortnight's leave, and being anxious that my family should be left at Simlah somewhat more comfortable than the few things they could carry on an ordinary dâk would make them, I determined to try how far it would be practicable to pack our traps on ekhas * loaded lightly; travelling in one myself, while my wife and two children, the youngest a baby of eight months old, went in a light phaeton, dragged and pushed by bearers.

We had sent on to Umritsur, forty-four miles, to endeavour to change the ekhas that brought us from Lahore, but none were procurable; the drivers, however, assured me that if I fed the ponies well, they were perfectly capable of carrying our party on to Jullundur; which distance from Lahore, upwards of ninety miles, they accomplished in thirty hours, arriving at Jullundur on the evening of the 29th.

* Country, or native pony carriages.

At Jullundur we had the choice of two roads to Simlah, the shorter one by Balachore, the other *via* Loodianah and Umballah; my own judgment would have led me to choose the more frequented but longer road, but the official who led the dak assured me that the Balachore road was not only shorter but preferable.

Unfortunately I was over-persuaded by what I thought was his local knowledge, versus only my opinion.

The rain had been falling heavily and the clouds were lowering. At 3 o'clock P.M., on the 30th of July, we started, and without mishap arrived within sight of Balachore by daylight. The Himalayas were looking very majestic; we began to think our *cicerone* right; all seemed *couleur de rose*: but on arriving at the staging bungalow, alas! all our hopes were dashed to the ground. A fat, and, strange to say, blue-eyed native official, of the Mahomedan tribe, rushed to the house to tell me that we must return immediately; and, if possible, by a cross and unfrequented road which led direct to Phillore, as, in consequence of some disturbance at Lahore, orders had just been received to destroy all the boats on the Sutlej, and that it was impossible we could cross at Rooper.

To me he imparted the additional pleasing intelligence that if, as he suspected, the regiments had mutinied at Lahore, they would, in all probability, make for Balachore.* The latter I did not at the time communicate to my wife, but the anxiety I felt at every moment's delay I cannot describe.

No sooner had we made preparations for a fresh start than the rain came down in torrents; a stream close to the bungalow became impassable, and the whole face of the country assumed the appearance of a lake.

At 2 o'clock P.M. the rain ceased; the river, which, like all streams near the Himalayas, fell as quickly as it rose, became passable, and we determined to make a start; anything I felt was better than remaining where we were, with the chance of falling into the hands of ruffians who never had shown mercy, even to women and children.

Although the stream had somewhat subsided, the waters were still deep; for ten miles I waded above my knees, the axles of the carriage being under water, never knowing for a moment that it might not be precipitated into some hidden stream or deep

* The 26th N. I. had the day before mutinied at Lahore, killed their colonel, and deserted in a body.

hole. To do the bearers who dragged the carriage, and the servants who accompanied us, justice, they worked like slaves; although poor creatures they had had little to eat, and saw little in the prospect to encourage them.

At one time I despaired of reaching our destination, and thought we must have stopped until the waters had become less. It became deeper and deeper, and at one time we had eight inches of water inside the carriage. Everything in the shape of clothing for the poor children was drenched, many things floated away, and the few biscuits we had for them were reduced to pulp.

Ladies under trying circumstances are far better sufferers than men. History cannot show greater heroism than they have evinced during this terribly eventful year, although in many cases tried to the utmost.

From the commencement of the mutiny, although surrounded by events calculated to excite alarm, not a murmur had I heard from her whose only thought was for the little ones who were so entirely dependent on her care.

By degrees we extricated ourselves from the lowlands near the river, and proceeded in comparative comfort for some hours, until night set in, and with it the rain began to fall. Thankful that the dear ones in the carriage, fairly exhausted, had fallen asleep, we pushed on slowly until about two o'clock in the morning; when, as a crowning point, the rain put out our torch, which, up to the present time we had, by dint of great care, preserved alight. Without its friendly aid it was impossible we could in any way proceed. In hopes that some village might be near, we all halloed for assistance. No response was given, the track was nowhere visible, and we determined to halt until the return of day. Each crouched where most shelter was procurable, to indulge in an hour's sleep.

As day dawned we discovered that it was indeed well we had halted. The ground for some distance had been slightly cut up, but further ahead it was a mass of ravines; the road, if so it could be called, taking a tortuous course through them, and in many places the water was very deep. We got on slowly, arriving at Phillore at twelve o'clock in the daytime. Here we found that the column, delayed by the very heavy rain, was just crossing the Sutlej. Colonel Dawes' troop of Horse Artillery had been ordered to remain in the Punjaub, much to their disappointment. Our friends supplied all our wants, and we arrived at Loodiana, at 9 P.M., to enjoy a night's

sound rest—a thing we had not known since leaving
Lahore.

Once again upon the beaten and frequented road,
our troubles were comparatively at an end.   We
started at 7 A.M. on the morning of the 2nd of
August, and arrived at the foot of the Himalayas on
the morning of the 4th, and at Simlah on the afternoon
of the 5th.

Having spent three happy and quiet days with my
family, and been enabled to settle them with every
comfort around them, I was obliged, on the morning
of the 8th, to make a rush down, calculating to catch
the column at Kurnal.

A couple of good strong ponies carried me forty-
four miles to the foot of the hills in eight hours.
There I learnt that General Nicholson had pushed on
by forced marches, and that I should have difficulty
in overtaking him.   Sooner would I have lost my
commission than have allowed my battery to march
into Delhi without me.

The good bustling old landlady of the Bull Inn,
at Kalka, " a thorough old soldier," sympathising
fully with my distress, fastened me down to cold
chicken and a bottle of beer, while she went out her-
self to raise the post-office officials to give me an express cart.   Her arguments and entreaties prevailed;

in she rushed with the glad tidings of her success, with the mail cart at her tail. In went the bundle, up I jumped, and after a severe fight with the ponies at starting, away we went at the rate of eleven miles an hour, over as rough and rocky a road as one could well imagine.

The first forty miles riding down the hills had taken it pretty well out of me; but the cart, devoid of its usual ballast in the shape of mail bags, fractured nearly every bone in my body. At 10 at night we arrived at Umballah, as the Loodiana cart with the mails from the north arrived at the post-office.

Little dreaming of any opposition to my onward progress, my bundle, as much bumped about as its master, was being transferred to the new vehicle, when a sable-countenanced apothecary appeared upon the stage, and at once disputed my right to the vacant seat, he having, as he stated, been waiting for three days. An argument, not of the gentlest kind, immediately sprang up as to whether the inflicter or healer of wounds was most urgently required at Delhi. He was positive that his advent would be hailed with joy, while that of a captain of artillery would be but a matter of indifference. Perhaps he was right: be that as it may, while he stormed I adjusted my seat and started, leaving my little black friend vowing that all sorts of pains and penalties should attach to my devoted person.

Nature borne up by strong excitement can bear an immense deal, particularly when the conviction is clear that a certain thing must be done. The first three stages of the road, from Umballah to the Markundah river, were so bad that sleep was out of the question, and even to hold on was a matter of difficulty; but beyond, where the road was well made, after three times rescuing me from falling from my perch, the driver found that it was impossible to keep me awake. A broken spring, to which previously he had appeared perfectly indifferent, was his excuse to transfer the mails and my sleeping self to a covered van, known as " a penny a miler;" the transfer I just remember, but nothing more, until the execrations of the driver at his done-up pony, awakened me to the fact that the once large but now deserted station of Kurnal was in sight. Here I had hoped to have found the column; but ignis-fatuus-like it had fled; my horses were laid upon the road for a twenty-mile ride: a cup of tea and a Newfoundland dog sort of shake was all I had time for. At 7 A. M. I again started, and found myself two hours afterwards at Paneeput with my old comrades, chattering round the mess-table of my battery, after travelling 168 miles in the preceding twenty-five hours; sixty-four miles having been done on horseback, the remainder on the mail cart.

We were now within sound of the guns at Delhi: morning, evening, and noonday, their thunder penetrated to our camp, and all were burning with anxiety to witness for ourselves what was the state of affairs and the position occupied by our force.

Some few of us thought we knew Delhi, but found afterwards how painfully slight was the knowledge of that wonderfully strong position. General Nicholson had preceded the column and gone into Delhi, sending back orders that on the following day (the 10th) we were to march to Lursowlee.

There were to be seen the first signs of that deadly struggle we were about to enter upon. The town was held for us by the Jheend Rajah, who had undertaken to keep open our communication towards the Punjaub. Across the road and extending far right and left were field-works furnished with guns. The Rajah's force being encamped within this line of defence.

On the 11th we halted at Lursowlee, to allow Captain Green's Punjaub regiment to swell our ranks, and on the following day encamped at

[8]   D

Raie, where General Nicholson again joined the column.

Expectation was on tiptoe to hear his opinion as to the state of affairs. He told me that the tide had turned, but that we should have some tough work; and that General Wilson had promised our column a little job, to try our " 'prentice hands," to dislodge a body of troops who had taken up their position with some guns in the neighbourhood of the Ludlow Castle.*

On the 12th we marched to Raie, and as we approached nearer, curiosity and expectation knew no bounds: a native trooper who came with letters from the camp, was squeezed dry of every idea he possessed. "Batteries," he said, "we should find extended further than the eye could reach, shot and shell were ordinary compliments, and a night's rest was a thing we none of us must again hope for."

The 13th brought us to Alipore, not more than seven miles from the camp; with our glasses we could discern the Flag-staff Tower on the top of the ridge, and at night the flashes of the guns, not few or far

---

* The guns proved so annoying to the troops at the Metcalfe picquet, and also to the camp that their capture could not be delayed. Brigadier Showers took the party completely by surprise, and brought four guns into camp.

between, told that they were "making a night of it."
Through our nasal organs we were most painfully
made aware of the scenes we were about to enter
upon. From Alipore to the camp, death in every
shape greeted our approach; even the trees, hacked
about for the camels' food, had a most desolate
appearance, throwing their naked boughs towards
heaven as if invoking pity for themselves or punishment on their destroyers.

A messenger was sent express to our camp to
intimate that we might expect an attack, and that
a force had been sent out from Delhi to prevent our
junction with General Wilson.

Nothing seemed more likely. Our greatest safety
from surprise was the state of the country: five
yards on either side of the road (except exactly
the ground on which we were encamped) was a
swamp, impracticable for artillery or cavalry; but
on this occasion, as in most others during the
mutiny when head and combination were necessary,
the enemy signally failed to take advantage of their
position.

Although fully prepared for an attack, none was
attempted. On the morning of the 14th of August,
having passed the strongly fortified position of Badul-
ke-serai, where the mutineers made their first stand

against the Commander-in-Chief, with our bands playing, and hearty cheers, we joined General Wilson's force, which had for so long a time withstood the brunt of the mutiny.

CHAPTER IV.

THE FORCE BEFORE DELHI.

The Delhi field force has been compared in many respects, on a small scale, to the allied armies before Sebastopol; in some points there is a resemblance: both drew their supplies and reinforcements from their rear, and from a great distance; each was unable, from its great inferiority in numbers, compared with the besieged, to invest the fortress; while in each case the besieged had the command of an unlimited supply of ordnance and ordnance stores.

The position of the army might more correctly have been called an entrenched camp, holding the forces within the city in check, and from time to time repelling their numerous sorties; keeping up a constant fire from a series of batteries erected on a long rocky ridge, which formed a natural protection to the front of the position, while on the right, at a high mound, was formed a strong picquet to protect that flank of the camp.

I write but of what took place at Delhi after our arrival, and therefore can give no detailed account of the numerous engagements which occurred prior to the arrival of the column; suffice it, that for the two first months, from the 8th of June to the beginning of August, seldom a day passed without either a real or a feigned attack: every detachment of reinforcements, as they joined, had to prove their fidelity to the Mahomedan cause by a decided engagement.

Yet, although so tremendously overpowering in numbers, but once did a few cavalry troopers penetrate into the camp, and few of them returned to tell the tale.

At the time we arrived things were remarkably quiet, and the morning and evening game at long bowls, was our only occupation; but still, although no further reinforcements were expected, it was necessary to wait for the siege train, now *en route* for Ferozepore, before the actual siege could be commenced upon.

General Wilson, from the time he took command on the 17th of July, had apparently determined to leave nothing to chance; he must have known full well that failure would be disastrous, not only to his force, but to India at large. The Punjaub, up to the present time tranquil, was in a state of vacillation; placards of an inflammatory nature were posted in every village; the Bombay army was shaky; a rising which cut off our postal communications with Bombay at Gogaira had already taken place; and, to use the words of the Judicial Commissioner in the Punjaub, "India seemed to be slipping through our fingers :" and so it was.

Every day's delay to the siege train was of vital importance; but a line of carts, eight miles long, travels slowly, and it was many days yet before it could be expected.

But to return to Delhi. General Wilson had determined to remain as much as possible on the defensive until the train arrived. The position was strengthened by connecting the batteries with walls on the ridge, and the ridge with the Subzie Mundie and Sammy-House, our right rear and right front posts, and providing more effectual cover for the guns and picquets.

The troops were relieved from duty as much as possible; no bugles, save the "turn out" and "alarm," were allowed, and then only as a preparatory measure; no movement was allowed without positive orders from the generals of division or their brigadiers.

Thus we found things at Delhi. Far from being in a dispirited state, as it was supposed, the greatest confidence as to the final result existed, and when off duty, there was no lack even of amusement: quoits, and sometimes foot-ball, in the head-quarters camp, made the evening pass merrily by.

The body of troops which left Delhi on the 13th or 14th, with the apparent view of preventing the junction of General Nicholson's force with the main army, was still unaccounted for; and as it was pretty certain they were up to some mischief, either by cutting off our communications with the Punjaub, or attacking our camp in the rear, Lieutenant Hodson, with a body of cavalry numbering about 300 sabres, was sent to watch their proceedings.

On the first morning he came upon a party of cavalry, who were surprised, and all but annihilated. He then pushed on for Rohtuck, and from the reports which reached the camp, serious apprehensions were entertained for his little band; they were happily unfounded. He returned on the 22nd August, after having dispersed and driven back towards Delhi the whole force; which had, it was discovered, been sent to raise revenue in the Rohtuck district.

The enemy were supplied with the best information, and were well aware that the train, which was but slightly escorted, was *en route* from Ferozepore.

On the 24th of August, a force, with about eighteen guns, was detached from the city to intercept its progress. This move from the " castle " was met by a " knight," who allowed no difficulties to hinder the attainment of his object.

With a column consisting of sixteen Horse Artillery guns, four squadrons of cavalry, and about 1,600 infantry; General Nicholson started on the morning of the 25th.

The track he had to travel was off the Grand Trunk Road, and on account of the deep swamps, all but impassable for artillery; but Tombs, who commanded that branch, had as little idea of an obstacle being insurmountable as the General himself.

In many places, axle-deep in water and mud, the guns had to be extricated by hand, and by dint of undaunted perseverance. I must here trespass on Major Norman's narrative for a detailed account of this enterprise and engagement.

" At Nangloe, nine miles from camp, intelligence was received of the enemy's movements, and the troops were immediately pushed on towards Nujjufghur. Arriving there at about four in the afternoon, the enemy were found occupying a position about a mile and three-quarters in length, extending from the canal bridge to the town of Nujjufghur. The baggage was left behind, protected by a detachment of the 2nd Punjaub Cavalry and 120 Punjaub Horse.

"The strongest point of the enemy's position was an old serai on their left, in which they had posted four guns; nine more were between the serai and the canal bridge.

"By 5 P.M. the troops were across the ford, and advanced to the attack of the serai; with the intention, after its capture, of sweeping down to the left, along the enemy's line, to the bridge.

"One hundred men from each corps formed the reserve. The 61st Foot, 1st Bengal Fusiliers, and 2nd Punjaub Infantry, were formed up with the Artillery on either flank, supported by the 9th Lancers and Cavalry of the Guide corps.

"After a few rounds from the guns, the Infantry charged, carried the position, changed front, and swept down the enemy's line. The rebels fled over the bridge, while the guns were playing on them. Thirteen pieces of artillery, with a large quantity of ammunition, was left in our hands.

"The 1st Punjaub Infantry cleared the town of Nujjufghur, and were sent to take a village in their rear; where the resistance was so obstinate, that the

61st Foot were sent back in support. The village
was evacuated during the night.

" The troops bivouacked upon the ground without
food, having been either fighting or marching all
day.

" The Sappers mined and blew up the Nujjufghur
bridge.

" The column returned to camp on the evening of
the 26th of August. The enemy, having quite given
up all idea of going to our rear, were in full retreat
on Delhi.

" On the morning of the 26th, the mutineers,
believing that the force left in camp after General
Nicholson's departure was very small, attacked the
right of the ridge, and opened guns from the
Ludlow Castle and a battery lately formed on the
opposite bank of the river.

" The attack was not of a serious nature, and was
soon repulsed, the enemy suffering much from the
Artillery fire.

" From information subsequently obtained, it is
certain that the King of Delhi, from the dates of
General Nicholson's junction with General Wilson,
and the loss of his guns at Nujjufghur only a few
days afterwards, felt that all chance of success
against the British force was at an end."

Such was the dread in which the wrath of this pseudo king was held, that the result of the Nujjuf-ghur expedition was for a time concealed from him, and a fictitious story circulated, that not only were their own guns being brought back by the country people, but those also which had been captured from the British; that scarcity of provisions had obliged them to return without their guns, which were delayed in consequence of the swampy state of the country.

This story, so improbable, was current but a short time; and when the truth came to light, the rage of the imbecile monster is said to have been excessive. The Commander, Bukht Khan,* a subadar of Artillery, who had been chief among the mutineers, and had raised the standard of rebellion in Rohilcund, was dismissed from the presence in disgrace. The Council was harangued in no measured terms as to their duplicity and unvaried failure in every attempt against the handful of British troops, and terms were sought, clandestinely, by members of the Royal family.

---

* Bukht Khan, like the Nana, was always very fond of English society. At one time, when studying Persian, he used to come twice a day to my house to read and talk with me. He was a most intelligent character, but a more dreadful hypocrite never stepped on earth.

The reply was the only one a British General could give. That it would be delivered at the ridge at a certain hour; at which time every gun opened upon the city, and told plainly the terms that might be expected.

CHAPTER V.

THE SIEGE AND CAPTURE OF DELHI.

THE first act of the Delhi tragedy may here be said to have terminated. The train was at hand, and to save a day's delay was of the utmost importance, not only to the country in general, but more especially to the Delhi Field Force.

The season was approaching when a low fever became prevalent, of a most debilitating nature; the hospitals were filling daily, more and more rapidly, and cholera seemed on the increase. On the 3rd of September, supported by two squadrons of the 9th Lancers, No. 17 Battery left Delhi for Rhei, distant about sixteen miles, to reinforce the Belooch Battalion, which formed the only escort to the siege train.

The stink of dead cattle along the road for the first seven miles, was even worse than when we came into Delhi three weeks before; the rest of the trip was like a holiday, the contrast of the fresh country air being grateful to the senses after the tainted atmosphere we had been inhaling.

We had not long to wait before the line of guns, howitzers, and mortar carts, chiefly drawn by elephants, soon "hove in sight," followed by a train of carts drawn by oxen, extending over a distance of eight miles, loaded with shot, shell, and ammunition of every kind and description. Poor "pandy," what a pounding was in store for you.*

At half-past 5 P.M. on the third, we started on our return to camp. It was a wearisome trip, but without adventure; the train was safely brought into camp on the morning of the 4th, when operations were commenced in earnest. About this time a far more destroying enemy than the enemy's shot and shell attacked my company. Cholera in its worst form broke out among them.

It was almost a matter of certainty that every corps as it arrived went through a course of this terrible disease. H. M.'s 52nd and 61st, who arrived at the same time, suffered also severely. The attacks of the disease seemed to justify the theory that certain

---

* From the adoption of the word pandy, as the cognomen of a mutinous sepoy in general, it has been supposed that the rising was acknowledged as a Hindoo insurrection; "pandy" being the designation of a caste of Hindoos. The first two men hung at Barrackpore were pandies by caste, hence all sepoys were pandies, and ever will be so called.

constitutions taking in a certain amount of miasma, the result was cholera and death. Hardly a man taken escaped, and out of seventy-five, in the course of a few days, seven were lying in the grave-yard.

Personally, I took little part in the work of the trenches. It was General Wilson's wish as much as possible to keep my Battery (No. 17) in reserve, to form part of the column which, immediately after the assault, was to follow the enemy in pursuit. This was an arrangement little to our minds, and I fear our feelings were of a kind little less mutinous than those of the sepoys within the city. In fact, I am not sure that it was not suggested that we should walk over to the enemy, battery and all. We were only told to obey orders, like good children; so we sulked quietly in our tents, or from the ridge watched the storm below.

The batteries on the ridge formed a base on which our siege operations commenced, and may be said not only to have formed a protecting rampart to our position, but a first parallel of investment; while a ravine running nearly parallel to it, and extending up to the Ludlow Castle, at a distance averaging from six to seven hundred yards from the walls, was our second parallel, and saved an immense deal of labour and loss of life.

The first operations were commenced early in September, prior to the arrival of the siege train. A trench was dug on the left of the Sammy House (our most advanced position on the right of the ridge), and in this trench a battery was erected for four 9-pounders and two 24-pounder howitzers, having for its object the prevention of sorties from the Lahore or Cabul Gates which, passing round the city walls, might have annoyed our breaching batteries, while at the same time it assisted in keeping down the fire of the Mooree Bastion.*

On the 6th of September, the last detachment which possibly could be expected had arrived in camp. The effective strength of the whole force, including Lascars, artillery drivers, and newly raised Sikh levies, amounted to 8,748, while 2,977 were sick in hospital, and the numbers of the latter were daily increasing.

The strength of the British troops was

Artillery	580
Cavalry	443
Infantry	2,294
In all	3,317

* Nearly the whole of the siege operations have been compiled from Major Norman's narrative, and "Felix," an engineer officer's account, published in the *Lahore Chronicle;* omitting only some minor details, and here and there amalgamating the information contained in each.

E

The native forces in camp amounted to 5,431. On their fidelity we could only depend so long as their interests were ours, and the prospect of plunder was before them; added to which, no support was nearer than Lahore, distant 300 miles. From this it will be seen that General Wilson's position was one to try the strongest nerves.

Felix thus describes the siege operations.

We had from the first no choice as to the front of attack; our position on the north side being the only one that could secure our communications with the Punjaub, whence our supplies had been drawn.

Whether the city might or might not have been carried by a *coup de main*, as was contemplated in June and July, is needless now to inquire. But, judging from the resistance afterwards experienced in the assault, though we were greatly reinforced, it appears fortunate that the attempt was not made.

The strength of the place had been greatly undervalued, and it was never supposed to consist in its actual defences. Every city is, from its nature, even when without fortifications, strongly defensible; and within Delhi the enemy possessed a magazine containing upwards of 200 guns, with an inexhaustible supply of small arms and ammunition of all sorts, while their numbers were never less than double those of the besiegers.

Few will doubt that the General exercised a sound discretion in refusing to allow a handful of men, unaided by siege guns, to attack such a place; knowing how disastrous would be a failure.

The Artillery force, at the commencement of the siege, consisted of

> Four Troops of Horse Artillery.
> Two Light Field Batteries.
> Forty heavy guns and howitzers.
> Ten heavy mortars.
> Twelve light mortars.

The means of the Engineers were very restricted, 120 trained sappers only being available; but with the aid of some companies of Sikhs newly raised and rapidly trained, and superintended by Lieutenant Brownlow with untiring energy and activity, 10,000 fascines, as many gabions, and 100,000 sandbags, together with scaling ladders, field magazines, and spare platforms, were prepared and ready for immediate use.

The north face being the side to be attacked, it was resolved to hold the right in check as much as possible, and to push the main attack on the left. 1st, as the river completely protected our flank as we advanced; 2ndly, as there was better cover on that side; and 3rdly, after the assault the troops would not immediately find themselves in narrow streets, but in comparatively open ground, on which to form.

The front to be attacked consisted of the Mooree, Cashmere, and Water Bastions, with the curtain walls commanding them. These walls had been greatly improved by our engineers, and presented a succession of faces and flanks, with regularly constructed embrasures. The curtain walls were twenty-four feet above the plain of site, eight feet of which was a mere parapet three feet thick, the remainder about twelve feet thick; outside the wall was a berm, and a ditch sixteen feet deep and twenty feet wide at the bottom. The escarp and counterscarp walls were steep; the latter unreveted, the former reveted with stone, eight feet in height. A glacis covered ten feet of the wall, rendering it impossible to breach that portion of it from any distance.

On the evening of the 7th of September, No. 1 Battery was traced in two portions, at a distance of about 700 yards from the Mooree Bastion: the right to contain five 18-pounders and one 8-inch howitzer, intended to silence the Mooree, and prevent its interfering with the left attack; the left portion for four 24-pounders, to hold the Cashmere Bastion partially in check.

Early on the morning of the 7th, both portions of this battery were completed and armed; its flanks being connected with the ravine in its rear, which protected the guards of the trenches, and the litters for the wounded and sick.

For some time the fire from the Mooree on this battery was most harassing, and also from musketry from a trench below the ridge; but as the guns came into full play, the enemy's fire was completely overpowered, and the Mooree on the 9th was but a mass of ruins. This battery was known as Brind's Battery, having been worked by Major Brind during the siege; or rather until, having done its work, its services were no more required: and, strange to say, only a few hours before dusk, when it was intended to dismantle the battery, the left portion was accidentally ignited, and utterly destroyed.

To our surprise we had been allowed to take possession of the Ludlow Castle, within six hundred yards of the city walls, without opposition; the enemy doubtless thinking that the assault was intended from the right, where our batteries had from the first been erected on the ridge; and the attack on the Mooree Bastion confirmed this belief.

On the 8th the Ludlow Castle and the Koodshah Bagh were occupied by strong detachments of infantry; Nos. 2 and 3 Batteries in front of Ludlow Castle, and on the left, were traced and commenced on the same evening, and on the morning of the 11th opened fire and were soon in full play.

No. 2 Battery, like Major Brind's, was constructed in two parts: one immediately in front of Ludlow Castle, for nine 24-pounders, to open a breach between the Cashmere and Water Bastions; and by knocking off the parapet right and left of the breach, to destroy all cover for musketry. The second portion was some two hundred yards to the right, in which were mounted seven 8-inch howitzers, and two 18-pounders; their object was to aid the left half of the battery and work to the same end.*

A flank was afterwards added, and in it an embrasure constructed for a heavy howitzer, intended to counteract the effect of guns brought by the enemy in the neighbourhood of the Kissengunge and Talewara suburbs.

The first salvo from this battery from nine 24-pounders showed what might soon be expected. The Cashmere Bastion attempted to reply, but was soon silenced, and became almost as great a wreck as its

---

* Major Campbell commanded the left half of No. 2 Battery, and Major Kaye the right. When Major Campbell was wounded on the evening of the 11th, Captain Johnson assumed command and held it until the assault.

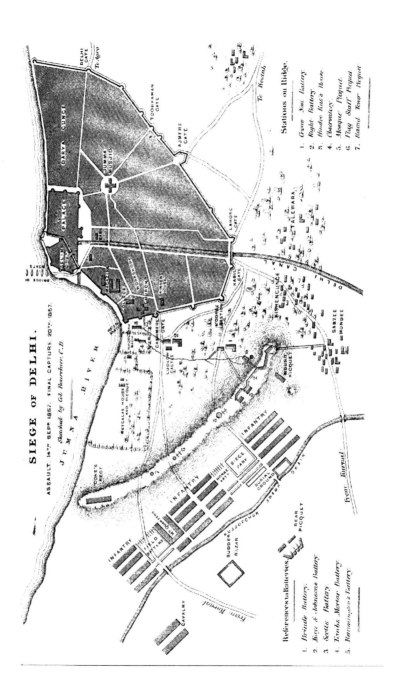

SIEGE OF DELHI.

ASSAULT 14TH SEPR 1857. FINAL CAPTURE 20TH 1857.

Sketched by Col. Bourcher, C.B.

Stations on Ridge.

1. Gone Noti Battery.
2. Right Battery.
3. Hindoe Rac's Hone.
4. Observatory.
5. Mosque Picquet.
6. Flag Staff Picquet.
7. Round Tower Picquet.

References to Batteries.

1. Brinde Battery.
2. Kaye & Johnsone Battery.
3. Scotts Battery.
4. Tombs Mortar Battery.
5. Remmington 2 Battery.

twin brother the Mooree; neither were portions of the curtain walls in a much better plight.

Simultaneous with the construction of No. 2 Battery, No. 3, on the extreme left, was commenced and executed in the boldest manner possible, within 180 yards of the Water Bastion, in which it was intended to form a breach. It was built behind a small ruined house in the Custom House compound, and under such a fire of musketry as few batteries have ever been exposed to. It was for six 24-pounders, which opened on the forenoon of the 11th, commanded by Major Scott, who most effectually performed his task.

No. 4 Battery, for ten heavy mortars, in the Koodshah Bagh, and some lighter ones behind the Custom House, opened on the 12th. The former were commanded by Major Tombs, the latter by Captain Blunt.

From this time until the moment of assault, the continuous roar of fifty guns and mortars pouring shot and shell into the devoted city, warned the enemy that retribution was coming on apace.

It must not be supposed that although no opposition was made to our occupation of Ludlow Castle and the Koodshah Bagh, that the batteries were unmolested.

On the night of the 8th, a sortie was made on No. 1 Battery; and although repulsed with slaughter to the enemy, yet it required constant showers of grape from Captain Remmington's battery at the Sammy House, to clear the broken ground of skirmishers; while guns which had been brought out from the city into the suburbs, enfiladed our line of batteries and did much mischief.

Three guns with the same view were in battery on the opposite side of the Jumna, and a continual fire was kept up from the Selimghur, a fort on the Jumna side of the city.

On two occasions, sallies were made from the Cashmere Gate before No. 2 Battery was in full play; and the heavy covering parties of infantry kept in the trenches were constantly at work keeping down the musketry fire, which was opened from a trench running parallel to, and three hundred yards from, our left attack, and was kept up until the morning of assault.

On No. 3 Battery, on the left, a tremendous fire of musketry was kept up from the city walls and the Water Bastion: the mantlets on the guns showed scarcely an inch without a dent. Captain Fagan, of the Artillery, whose gallantry and energy had won for him the admiration of every officer in camp, was killed by a musket-ball through the head, while looking over his gun to see the effect of the fire. A kind friend and a gallant soldier, his loss was deeply felt by all who that evening followed him to the grave.

CHAPTER VI.

THE ASSAULT AND CAPTURE OF DELHI.

So well had affairs been conducted in camp, that although naturally enough every one was aware that the time for the assault was at hand, it was late on the night of the 13th before (the breaches having been declared practicable) orders were issued for the assault on the following morning. All necessary preparations were at once made, and at 4 A.M. of the 14th of September—a day none present will forget— four columns were collected at their respective parades, preparatory to moving to the attack. They were composed as follows :—

First column commanded by Brigadier-General Nicholson, to storm the breach near the Cashmere Bastion, and escalade its face.

H. M.'s 75th . .	.	300
2nd Punjaub Infantry	. .	450
1st Bengal Fusiliers .	. .	250
Total .	. .	1,000

Second column, Brigadier Jones, C.B., to storm the breach in the Water Bastion.

H. M.'s 8th	. . . .	250
2nd Bengal Fusiliers .	. .	250
4th Sikh Infantry	. . .	350
Total	. . .	850

Third column, Colonel G. Campbell, H. M.'s 52nd, to assault by the Cashmere Gate after it should be blown open.

H. M.'s 52nd	. . . .	200
Kumaon Battalion	. . .	250
1st Punjaub Infantry	. .	500
Total	. . .	950

Fourth column, Major Reid, Sirmoor Battalion, to attack the Kissen Gunge from the ridge, and enter the city by the Lahore Gate. This column consisted of the Sirmoor Battalion and Guides, with the picquets from the ridge: strength about 850. Besides these, there was the Cashmere Contingent.

Fifth column (the reserve), Brigadier Longfield.

H. M.'s 61st	. . . .	250
4th Punjaub Infantry	. .	450
Belooch Battalion	. . .	300
Jheend Force	. . . .	300
H. M.'s 60th Rifles	. . .	200*
		1,500

* H. M.'s 60th Rifles had for some days been in the advanced batteries covering the artillery, and keeping down the musketry fire of the walls. This regiment covered the advance of the storming columns.

This column subsequently was brought into the city after the assault.

Three Engineer officers were attached to each column, and it was intended that a couple of guns should have accompanied each also; but the draw-bridges being broken, the guns were drawn up near the Ludlow Castle.

The morning was still and sultry; not a sound was to be heard save the continued roaring of the batteries, which to the last poured their deadly salvos into the city. General Nicholson, who at his especial request was selected to lead the assault, soon passed on to the road leading to the Cashmere Gate, and was followed by the remainder. It was the last time I ever saw him, and knowing the honourable but terribly dangerous post he had selected, as we shook hands, I felt that we had parted for life.

It seems a pity that a man with such administrative capacity was allowed to do what fifty others would have done equally well, and whose loss would have been less a national calamity. Felix thus admirably describes the assault:—

"Everything was ready. Nicholson, whose excellent arrangements elicited the admiration of all, gave the signal. The Rifles dashed to the front with a

cheer, extending along and skirmishing through the
low brushwood which extends to within fifty yards
of the ditch.   At the same moment the head of No. 1
and 2 columns emerged from the Koodshah Bagh,
and advanced steadily towards the breach.

"Our batteries had maintained a tremendous fire
up to the moment of the advance of the troops; and
not a gun could the enemy bring to bear on the
advancing columns.   No sooner did they emerge
into the open, than a perfect storm of bullets met
them from the front and flanks, and both officers
and men fell fast on the crest of the glacis.

"For ten minutes it was impossible to get ladders
into the ditch to ascend the escarp.   The determina-
tion of British soldiers carried all before it, and
Pandy declined to meet the bayonet.   With a cheer
and a rush the breaches were won, and the enemy
fled in disorder.

"In the meantime the explosion party advanced in
front of the three columns, straight upon the Cashmere Gate.*   This band of heroes (for they were no
less) had to advance, in daylight, to the gateway in
the very teeth of a hot fire of musketry from all sides.

* On arriving at the Cashmere Gate a horrible sight awaited
them; a European soldier (doubtless a prisoner) had been chained
outside the gate, and been killed by the shot from our batteries.

The powder bags were coolly laid and adjusted, but Lieutenant Salkeld was *hors de combat*, with two bullets through his body.

" Sergeant Carmichael attempted to fire the fuse, but was shot dead. Sergeant Burgess then attempted it and succeeded, but paid for the daring act with his life. Sergeant Smith, thinking that Sergeant Burgess had failed, ran forward ; but seeing the train alight, had just time to throw himself into the ditch and escape the effects of the explosion. With a loud crash the gateway was blown in, and through it the third column rushed to the attack, at the same moment that the other columns had won the breaches. General Wilson has since bestowed the Victoria Cross on Lieutenant Salkeld, Lieutenant Home, Sergeant Smith, and on a brave soldier of H. M.'s 52nd, who stood by Lieutenant Salkeld to the last, and bound up his wounds."

So far, all was as successful as could be wished— both breaches and the Cashmere Gate were in our hands. But a scene was passing outside that no pen can properly describe. For the reasons before assigned, General Wilson had ordered the light artillery which he had intended to accompany the columns, to form as much protection as possible near the Ludlow Castle. It was, indeed, a time of breathless anxiety.

The breaching batteries, having done their deadly work, had ceased; nothing but the continued rattle of musketry was heard, save the booming of the guns from the Selimghur Fort. The long, long line of litters commenced to return to the Field Hospitals from the scene of strife, with their mangled burthens; the dead, dying, and wounded in every state, were passing by, showing how deadly was the struggle. Though little separated from the scene of action, none could tell us what had been doing, or what was the state of affairs. Over and over again the same questions were asked, " Were the columns inside ? Were the breaches gained?" None could reply. The intense anxiety of that hour made it like a week, until that cheer which no Englishman can mistake proclaimed that the victory was ours, and that the day of retribution was at hand.

Major Norman thus describes the operations within the city, after the actual assault :—

Nos. 1 and 2 columns having effected an entrance, proceeded round the walls to the right, capturing a small battery and tower between the Cashmere and Mooree Bastion, the Mooree Bastion itself, and the Cabul Gate.

All attempts to take the Burn Bastion and Lahore Gates failed.

The troops had to advance up a narrow lane swept by grape and musketry; and in one of these attempts General Nicholson received his mortal wound.

Up to the Cabul Gate our position was secured, and the Artillery on the Mooree Bastion turned upon the city and Kissen Gunge suburbs; the gorge being secured by sandbag parapets.

The 3rd column, after storming the Cashmere Gate, proceeded through the town towards the Jumma Musjid. It was conducted most gallantly by Sir T. Metcalfe, who had voluntered for the service; his local knowledge being of the greatest assistance. Taking a circuitous route, little opposition was met with, until reaching the Chandnee Choke, possession was taken of the city police station.

The lanes leading to the Jumma Musjid here became more intricate, and the men began to fall fast. It was found impossible to capture the Musjid; the gates being strongly closed, and neither artillery nor powder-bags being at hand.

This column eventually fell back to the neighbourhood of the church; which, with the adjoining buildings, it occupied with the reserve.

Major Reid, with the 4th column, had in the mean time advanced from the Subzi-Mundi into the Kissen Gunge, the Cashmere Contingent operating on his

right.   The latter, however, were so sharply attacked
by the insurgents, that after losing a great number
of men* and four guns, they were completely defeated, and fell back to camp.

The most strenuous opposition was offered to
Major Reid's column in the Kissen Gunge.   Many
men and officers were *hors de combat;* the enemy
were strongly posted among gardens and walled
enclosures.   The commanding officer being severely
wounded, Captain Muter, of H. M.'s 60th Rifles, the
next senior, withdrew to the ridge; covered by the
guns which had been left in the Crow's Nest Battery
on the extreme right.

Brigadier Grant, with the cavalry and Horse
Artillery, effectually prevented any annoyance to
the flanks of the assaulting columns; but suffered
so severely from the guns and musketry in the
suburbs, that General Wilson ordered No. 17 Battery to move up in support and aid Major Tombs'
troop, which, with that officer's usual gallantry, had
been in the thick of the engagement, and suffered
so severely in men and horses that it was with difficulty he could drag his guns from the ground when
relieved.   The steadiness of the 9th Lancers and

---

* The number of casualties in the Cashmere Contingent is not
known.   They are not included in the return of casualties.

[8]   F

Carbineers was the subject of admiration. File after file was shot down; yet, in the quaint language of General Grant's despatch, " the spirits of the men seemed to rise as their ranks were thinned."

Gradually the fire of the Kissen Gunge became less, as the heavy guns from the Mooree Bastion were brought to bear on that quarter; and in the afternoon, it having nearly ceased, and no fears being entertained of an attack from that direction, General Grant's force was withdrawn to the Ludlow Castle, with picquets towards the ridge.

Thus ended the siege and assault of Delhi. The actual loss on the day of assault, in killed and wounded, was 66 officers and 1,104 men: nearly one-third of the number engaged; while the casualties which occurred from the opening of the batteries to the moment of assault, amounted to 327 officers and men. The loss to the enemy must have been severe. The best idea was the one which could be formed from the statement of Colonel Burn, the military governor of Delhi, that when he commenced to try and clear the houses, he seldom came upon one in which there were not eight or nine dead bodies.

For the complete success that attended the prosecution of the siege, the chief credit is due to Colonel Baird Smith, the chief engineer; and to

Captain Taylor, on whom, consequent on the former being early wounded, devolved the superintendence of the attack. The plan of the attack was bold and skilful. The nature of our enemy was exactly appreciated. Pandy can fight well behind walls, but here he was out-manœuvred: his attention was directed from the real point of attack until the last moment, when the cover, which would have been of such annoyance to us, had been seized and turned against him.

To enable the siege batteries to be fully armed, most of the heavy guns had been withdrawn from the ridge. Such only were left as would secure the position, while two light guns were, on the morning of the assault, added to the rear picquet.

The Foot Artillery, though never once relieved from the commencement of the actual siege, were quite insufficient to work the whole of the heavy ordnance: nearly all the officers and men of the Horse Artillery were sent into the batteries; these even were insufficient, and parties of volunteers from H. M.'s 9th Lancers and 6th Dragoon Guards, hastily trained, rendered most hearty and valuable service, while many officers, having undergone previously an apprenticeship on the ridge, rendered important assistance.

Not a man on the batteries was once relieved from the time of opening fire until the assault. In like manner the Engineers and Sappers were continually under fire, and without relief.

The 14th of September ended, if not with the full success that was anticipated, certainly with as much as the handful of troops engaged had a right to expect.

CHAPTER VII.

FIGHTING WITHIN THE CITY.

ALTHOUGH the first day's operations were most satisfactory, yet on the evening of the 14th September nothing but the city walls and bastions, extending from the Cabul Gate to the Water Bastion, and the open space round the church, college, and Skinner's house, were in our hands; and it was clear that the enemy intended to dispute every street, foot by foot, with us.

Unfortunately, that terrible license invariably consequent on the capture of a besieged city, was deeply indulged in. At the very entrance were large stores filled with wine, beer, and spirits, in the greatest abundance; and for a time, our tenure of the position we had gained was deeply imperilled. Our guard fell victims to their vice, and were all murdered at their posts; while champagne was taken by the followers outside the city to the Ludlow Castle and sold for about 3d. a bottle.

The most vigorous efforts were at once made to destroy all the liquor in the town. Thousands of dozens were broken up by guards placed at the disposal of the Provost-Marshal, and order was once more restored. Yet although the passions of the troops were, by drink and revenge, worked up to burning heat, not a case, it is believed, was heard of a woman or child having been intentionally hurt —all credit to them.

No sooner was the Cashmere gate open* than a tide of women and children poured out towards the British camp: a noble testimony of the estimate they placed on the national character. For hours and hours the stream passed up the Ludlow Castle road; the numbers were such that their remaining in or near the camp was impossible, and a large deserted village was told off for their especial use. Although the women and children were protected by the British, their own relatives and friends set much less value on their lives. We had adopted an ingenious method of discovering whether in the next street there were any riflemen, by putting out a hat at the corner on the point of a bayonet; it seldom returned without

---

* Several men were caught going out of the Cashmere Gate disguised as women, and were hung; while several bheesties, or water-carriers, detected bringing in drugged liquor for the troops, were likewise disposed of.

a bullet in it. These ruffians, trusting to the Europeans not firing at them, generally pushed forward a woman or a child as a feeler. Near the Lahore Gate this was especially remarkable, and it is only wonderful that several were not shot.

Although much delayed in advancing by the conduct of the troops, the 15th did not find us idle. The guns and mortars of the Mooree Bastion kept up a fire upon the city; others were brought into position for the same purpose; while the Water Bastion and a battery erected at the left of the college garden were opened upon the Selimghur, and two guns of Major Scott's battery made a breach in the magazine walls from the college square. The church, which was exposed to heavy fire from Selimghur, was also put into a more defensible state; the ordnance and engineering stores being brought within the churchyard enclosure.

On the morning of the 16th, the magazine was stormed and carried; but every building was fought for.

Towards the afternoon, an attempt was made to recapture it, as also the adjoining workshops, covered by the fire of some guns placed in front of the palace gate.

As far as the workshops were concerned, it was partially successful; but the enemy were soon driven off, and endeavoured, as they retired, to set fire to the roofs with torches.

Lieutenant Renny, of the Artillery, on this occasion exhibited the greatest coolness and gallantry, by mounting the roof and pelting the enemy with shells; which were handed up to him, with fuses alight. On the same morning, the Kissen Gunge was evacuated, being entirely commanded by the guns from the walls: naturally a strong position, every means had been taken to improve it; and it was indeed fortunate that we were not obliged to dislodge the enemy from the numerous fortified positions it contained. It would only have been done with great loss.

On the 18th, our positions were advanced in the centre, towards the canal; and on the left, the Bank House was taken possession of. The line of the canal may be said to have been our front: on its bank some light mortars were posted, to clear the neighbourhood of the Lahore Gate; while light guns were posted at the main junctions of the streets, and sandbag batteries erected to prevent the possibility of a surprise.

The whole of the heavy mortars were at work in the magazine, pouring a continuous flight of shells into the city and palace; and it became apparent that, although no post was given up uncontested, the resistance was becoming less, and that the abandonment of the city had commenced.

On the 19th, the Burn Bastion was captured; and on the following morning, the Lahore Bastion (which had twice before resisted our attacks) was assaulted, and, together with the remainder of the city walls, was held by our troops.

A column, hastily formed, pushed along the Chandnee Choke, and took possession of the Jumma Musjid, which was but slightly defended. A second was formed at the magazine, for a simultaneous attack upon the Palace. When the latter arrived at the gateway, the Palace was found to have been evacuated; save by a few fanatics, who fired from the walls, and were subsequently bayoneted by the troops. The gates were blown open, and General Wilson's head-quarters were there established. The Selimghur Fort had likewise been evacuated; a royal salute was fired from its ramparts, and the British flag was flying from the Palace walls.

Thus ended one of the most severe struggles history has on record. At the first it was the passive resistance of a handful against crowds of enemies. Our force, it must be remembered, had to contend with every disadvantage, not only of climate and sickness, but of circumstances of a still more discouraging nature. Reinforcements of every kind for the enemy were arriving day by day, crossing the bridge of boats before our eyes; but it was so far distant that the destruction of the bridge was impossible: several attempts to burn it were made, but in vain. Disastrous accounts were also received as to the state of the country. Mutiny after mutiny, massacre after massacre, were recorded; and the storm about July loomed so black, that it appeared certain nothing but Providence could save the vessel of the State.

Yet, under these circumstances, the little band before Delhi never desponded. All behaved nobly; but it may be permitted to allude to those corps most constantly engaged—the 60th Rifles, the Sirmoor Battalion, and the Guides Corps. Probably not one day throughout the siege passed without a casualty in one of these regiments. But the losses in action, compared with their original strength, show the nature of the service.

The Rifles commenced with 440 of all ranks, and a few days before the assault they received a reinforcement of 200: their casualties were 389.

The Sirmoor Battalion commenced 450 strong, and were reinforced by 90 men: its casualties amounted to 319.

The Guides Corps, 550 strong, lost 303 of their number.

The 1st Bengal Fusiliers, and, in fact, all the regiments, were severe losers. The 52nd, which arrived in Delhi only a month before the assault 600 strong, could only muster out of hospital on the day of assault 242 men of all ranks.

It only remains to say something of the appearance of Delhi on entering after the assault.

The demon of destruction seemed to have enjoyed a perfect revel. The houses in the neighbourhood of the Mooree and Cashmere Bastions were a mass of ruins; the walls near the breaches were cracked in every direction, while the church was completely gutted and riddled by shot and shell: its gilt cross was still untouched, and, as seen of a bright morning from the ridge, glittering in the rising sun, seemed beckoning us onwards, with the full assurance that the religion of the Cross should still, even in that city, soar high over Mahomedan bigotry and cruelty. In the Water Bastion the destruction was still more striking. Huge siege guns, with their carriages, lay about seemingly like playthings in a child's nursery. The Palace had evidently been hastily abandoned. The tents of Captain De Teissier's battery, stationed at Delhi when the mutiny broke out, were left standing, and contained plunder of all sorts.

The apartments inhabited by the royal family combined an incongruous array of tawdry splendour, with the most abject poverty and filth. The apartments over the Palace gate, formerly inhabited by Captain Douglas, who commanded the Palace guards, and Mr. Jennings, the clergyman, were denuded of every trace of the unfortunate party which had inhabited its walls; and with whom, not many months before, I had spent a happy week. It was with a sad and heavy heart that I paced its now empty rooms, which could tell such terrible tales of the scenes there enacted.

On the morning of the 21st of September, the cleansing of the city was commenced. Although previously every effort had been made to destroy the dead bodies, it was in a dreadful state. A military governor was appointed, guards were distributed, the light artillery were withdrawn to Ludlow Castle, and No. 17 Battery received orders to leave Delhi, under the command of Colonel Greathed.

The following is the return of killed, wounded, and missing of the Delhi Field Force, from the commencement of the operations on the 30th of May, 1857, to the final capture of the city on the 20th of September :—

Palace of Delhi, 23rd Sept., 1857.

KILLED.

Officers, European	46
„ Native	14
Non-commissioned Officers, European	35
„ „ Native	25
Drummers, &c., European	5
„ „ Native	2
Rank and File, European	476
„ „ Native	389

Total 992

Horses 139

WOUNDED.

Officers, European	140
„ Native	49
Non-commissioned Officers, European . . .	108
„ „ Native	99
Drummers, &c., European	5
„ „ Native	5
Rank and File, European	1,313
„ „ Native	1,076

Total 2,795

Horses 186

MISSING.

Non-commissioned Officers, Native	1
Rank and File, European	12
„ „ Native	17

Total 30

Horses 53

TOTAL KILLED, MISSING, AND WOUNDED.

Officers and Men . . . 3,817
Horses 378

CHAPTER VIII.

PROCEEDINGS OF THE COLUMN OF PURSUIT
FROM DELHI TO CAWNPORE.

NEVER did boys escape from the clutches of a school-
master with greater glee than we experienced on
the 21st of September, when we received our orders
to proceed on the following morning to the plain in
front of the Ajmere Gate, where a column was to
be formed under the command of Colonel Greathed,
H. M.'s 8th Foot, destined to scour the Gangetic
Doab. Its presence would restore confidence, by
instilling into the native mind the fact that not only
had the siege of Delhi come to an end, but that
British rule was again in the ascendant; by admi-
nistrating "vindicatory justice" upon those who
had aided and abetted in the rebellion; and also
bringing to battle the brigades of mutineers who
were attempting to cross the Doab, like rats escaping
from the empty house, and pushing their way
towards Cawnpore and Oude.

The trouble taken by these ruffians to impress upon the country the belief that the fall of Delhi was a fable, was most successful. It was long ere the provinces could realise the fact that the imperial city was in possession of the handful of British which had invested it.

The neighbourhood of Delhi and Meerut, for years notorious as the hot-bed of dacoity and misrule, was now a scene of anarchy.

The Goojah tribes, by whom unheard-of atrocities had been committed on the unhappy fugitives who escaped the fangs of the Palace officials and sepoy assassins of Delhi, were still in open rebellion; and a roving commission, with unlimited powers and martial law, was the only likely method of bringing the Doab into subjection. Well had it been if Colonel Greathed had been able to exercise these powers: as assuredly was intended. The civil power, which at the first outset of the mutiny in the North-West had suddenly collapsed, sprung up with mushroom-like rapidity the moment the column crossed the Jumna. Villages tainted with rebellion and murder were spared, only from fear that the coffers of the State might suffer a temporary deficit.

It remains to be decided whether any deficit would not have been preferable to allowing the whole country to be infested with gangs of villains who had witnessed the tragedy of the mutiny, or who, having been released from gaol by thousands, joined in its horrors.

So well known was the state of the country, that not a civilian would venture beyond the sound of our trumpets. Ere many days had passed, however, Mussulmen armed to the teeth, appeared at every village: men who, from their position and creed, could not have existed during the crisis, but as bowing the knee before the Mahomedan idol they had set up, now appeared as our devoted slaves.

The troops detailed to form the columns were as follows:—

	Europeans.	Native.
Captain Remmington's Troop of Horse Artillery, 5 guns	60	—
Captain Blunt's Troop of Horse Artillery, 5 guns	60	—
Bourchier's Battery, 6 guns	60	60
Sappers	...	200
H. M.'s 9th Lancers	300	—
Detachments 1st, 4th, 5th Punjaub Cavalry, and Hodson's Horse	...	400
European Infantry, H. M.'s 8th and 75th	450	—
Punjaub Infantry, 1st and 4th Regiments	...	1,200
Total of each	930	1,860
Grand total	2,790	

The column broke ground on the morning of the 24th of September, bidding adieu to the "city of the dead." Our road from the Ajmere Gate to the bridge lay through the Lahore Gate, and passing along the Chandnee Choke.

Not a sound was heard save the deep rumble of our gun wheels, or the hoarse challenge of a sentry on the ramparts. Here might be seen a house gutted of its contents, there a jackal feeding on the half demolished body of a sepoy; arms, carts, shot, dead bodies lay about in the wildest manner. Out-stretched and exposed to the public gaze, lay the bodies of the two sons and grandson of the wretched King; they had been captured and executed the day before near Humayoon's Tomb. The King's life, however, was guaranteed to him. The sight was one to be remembered: it was the first step towards that vengeance which Providence has ordained against those who, so foully and with treachery of the blackest dye, had broken his laws.

But, let us pause a moment and consider, was it ever to be expected that Mussulmen, after it suited their interests, would keep faith with those whom they consider infidels; when to be instrumental in their destruction is a meritorious act in the eyes of their accursed religion? The only comfort one of these miscreants possessed was to this effect: " I die happy: I have seen English women polluted in the streets of Delhi."

[8]   G

The air of the city seemed dense and uncomfortable to breathe; but the bridge once crossed, every moment brought us into a fresher atmosphere. It was wonderful in how short a time the spirits of all were raised by the change. Major Turner, who commanded the Artillery of the column, and who had suffered severely from the sun and fever during his exposure in the batteries, told me that the delight of escaping into fresh air made him inclined to sing.

But to return to our route. Our first march was to the banks of the river Hindun; it was crossed by a suspension bridge, which early in the campaign had been partially destroyed by our engineers to cut off that line of communication between Delhi and Meerut, and afterwards most ingeniously repaired by the rebels.

Our encamping ground was at Gazeeoodeen Nugger, General Wilson's first battle field, when, leaving Meerut early in June, he effected a junction with the Commander-in-Chief. Our mission was indeed a noble one: in fact nothing more or less than again taking possession of the country which had slipped from our grasp.

It has been well said that for months we possessed no territory in the North-West below Delhi and

Meerut, except just the ground on which our troops were encamped. Such indeed was the fact. The town of Gazeeoodeen Nugger was deserted, and the inhabitants of the village had fled, knowing what they ought to expect; and, conscience stricken, they doubted whether we came as friends or foes.

Our baggage cattle, which had for so long a period been on scanty and bad forage in Delhi, were in bad condition: the camels especially could scarcely carry their loads, and many died daily. It was the evening of our first march before the whole had arrived in camp, and it was necessary, in consequence, to halt the following day. It being found that the camels were overloaded chiefly from the quantity of plunder and trash that the camp followers had brought out of Delhi, a certain time was given them to dispose of the surplus loads; after which a search was ordered, and whatever was found in the shape of plunder was burnt.

On the 26th, with a sensible difference in the baggage, our camp moved to Dadra. There a quantity of property belonging to Europeans was found concealed in the villages; and as the inhabitants had been notoriously disaffected, the villages (which had been deserted previous to our arrival) were burnt.

Our next march was Secundra, only the previous

day evacuated by a body of cavalry detached from Walidad Khan's force at Malaghur Fort, which had for months been held by the rebels.

The town and surrounding villages were in a terrible plight. The inhabitants, quiet cultivators of the land, and a race opposed to the Goojahs, flocked out to meet us and to implore our protection. Every house had been gutted and destroyed; their property of every kind taken, and their bullocks, the only means of drawing water for irrigation purposes, driven away.

It was no difficult matter to discover who were for us and who were against us. The British rule brought peace to the labourer, while its discipline controlled the savage propensities of the Mussulman; who, while to gain his end he would invariably cringe in abject, nay loathsome, servility before his master, yet let him but attain his object and a little power, and he will twirl his moustaches and laugh in his sleeve at the credulity of those who fancy that aught but interest and pay kept him in the employment of Feringhee heretics.

On the morning of the 28th, we left Secundra for Bolundshur, a civil station forty-two miles from Meerut, and about five from the fort of Malaghur.

From the latter place it was to have been our

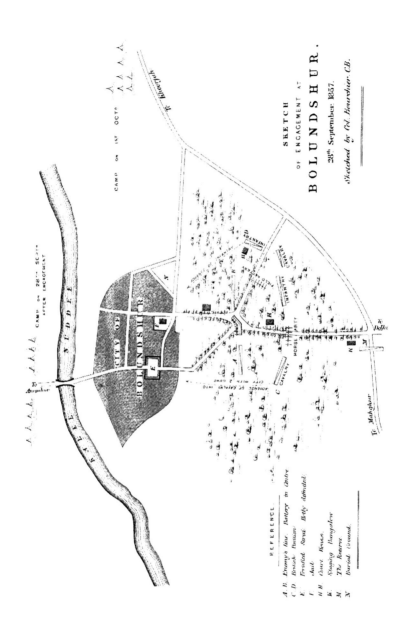

SKETCH

OF ENGAGEMENT AT

BOLUNDSHUR.

28th September 1857.

Sketched by Col. Bourchier C.B.

REFERENCE

A B   Enemy's line. Battery in Centre
C D   Brick Bridges
E   Fortified Serai Batty demoled.
I   Jail
H H   Court Houses.
K   Staging Bungalow
M   The Reserve
N   Burial Ground.

business to unearth Mr. Walidad, a relation of the
King of Delhi, and make him pay the penalty of
his sins.

About daylight the advanced guard arrived at
four cross roads about a mile and a half from
Bolundshur; one of which led to Malaghur,
another straight ahead to the civil station and
town.

A picquet of the enemy's cavalry which had been
placed on the junction fell back at our approach, and
it was ascertained that they had possession of the
station in force, and intended there to make a stand;
having their guns in battery commanding the entrance,
the houses, gardens, and offices being occupied by
the infantry, while bodies of horse were hovering
about, ready for any mischief that might turn up.

The advanced guard was strengthened by two of
Captain Remmington's Horse Artillery guns, and
were soon within range of the enemy; who opened at
once down the road. The column in the mean time
were being collected well in hand. A reserve was
formed, under command of Major Turner, at the
junction of the four roads before alluded to, for the
protection of the baggage; which was, as anticipated,
attacked in flank by cavalry and guns. These
were quickly driven off with loss; the infantry were

formed, and the artillery collected on the left of the road.

Remmington had not been idle: his two guns had opened on the enemy, and he was reinforced by the remainder of his troop; while my battery took up its position more to the right, supported by a squadron of Punjaub Cavalry, and a portion of H. M.'s 75th.

The enemy were not slow in turning a portion of their attention towards us, and plied their guns with a will; while from the high crops and the surrounding gardens a sharp fire of musketry was kept up. The infantry, forming on the right and centre, commenced an advance among the gardens. This was exactly the style of fighting Pandy enjoyed; his guns behind walls and his infantry concealed, while the attacking force was necessarily exposed at every step.

By the cross fire which was kept up upon the enemy's battery, their fire was subdued; an advance was then ordered. A few salvoes of grape cleared the front, and the commanding officer being anxious that the position should be secured, ordered an immediate advance of the artillery. Lieutenant Roberts, of the Artillery, who seemed ubiquitous, brought the order at a gallop. The guns charged and took the battery, the enemy scampering before us as we came up to it. Lieutenant Roberts was first at the guns. A second burst, after clearing our front with grape, brought us to the goal; the enemy flying before us like sheep.

While affairs had thus been successful on the right, a second column, consisting of the greater portion of the cavalry, with two guns of Captain Blunt's troop, under Lieutenant Cracklow, were busy on the left; and having advanced into the town, were for some time exposed to a most severe fire in the streets. Four men out of one gun's crew were wounded, and the gun was worked with difficulty. The conduct of the cavalry was conspicuous: under most disadvantageous circumstances they charged and defeated several bodies of the enemy far their superior in numbers.

The 9th Lancers, under Major Curry and Captain Drysdale, cleared the town. Their loss alone was three officers wounded, six rank and file and twenty-one horses *hors de combat*, before they extricated themselves from their position.

Three guns, an immense quantity of baggage and ammunition fell into our hands; and had the localities been better known, the loss to the enemy would have been much more severe, and the pursuit more speedily followed up: as it was, not fewer than three hundred could have fallen.

The action commenced about 7 A.M. and terminated at about 11, when the camp was pitched on the Annoopshur road, on the banks of the Kalee Nuddy. The fort of Malaghur was reconnoitred, and the cause of the stand at Bolundshur became apparent under its cover; the fort had been evacuated, and Walidad had made good his retreat to the Ganges!

A few guns of native manufacture were taken in the fort, from which a royal salute was fired, and a large manufactory of gunpowder was destroyed. Guncarriages were being built, and models of guns were on the lathes ready for casting. The place was crammed with stores, plunder, and furniture of every description; the property of officers who were at the station when the mutiny broke out, or which was in transit to the North-West.

Preparations were made for destroying one of the bastions of the fort by mining, which was most effectually carried out on the morning of the 1st of October; but, in superintending the operation, Lieutenant Home, of the Engineers, was unfortunately blown up and killed on the spot. He was one of those officers who so greatly distinguished himself on the morning of the assault of Delhi, by igniting the train which blew open the Cashmere Gate, under a heavy fire, and had been promised the Victoria Cross for his gallant conduct. His untimely death cast a gloom over the whole camp. The exact cause of the accident is not known; it is supposed that he used a native-made portfire to ignite the train, a spark from which may [have ignited the mine itself. Only the morning before we had been standing together unpacking powder stowed on carts in every shape imaginable, from the carefully packed barrel with four hoops fresh from the Delhi magazine, to loose cartridges and powder strewed all over the place; and close by, two men of the dragoons were quietly sitting smoking their pipes, while they were examining different articles in the carts. Poor Home's invective at their conduct, and the careless manner in which powder was generally handled, makes me feel sure that the unexpected explosion of the mine was the effect of accident, which no care on his part could have prevented.

On the morning of the 2nd of October the camp was shifted to the Allyghur road, and a proper escort having been secured, the sick and wounded were sent into Meerut.

On the 3rd the column marched to Koorjah, the

junction of the Delhi and Meerut roads—a town said
to have been the hotbed of mutiny. If the fact of
the utter destruction of Secundra and plunder of its
inhabitants was a sign that they had no sympathy
with the mutineers, the perfect protection afforded
to the town of Koorjah was evidence of a contrary
state of things. As the column entered, a tall Mahomedan subadar, formerly of the Gwalior Contingent,
and now a pensioner of the Government, came forth
to meet us, mounted on his well-conditioned and
caparisoned steed, his whole appearance displaying
the consummate insolence of his race ; he was known,
by many officers formerly connected with Gwalior,
as a most influential member of that force (now in
open mutiny, and which had at Gwalior perpetrated
such atrocities), and to be able, if required, to raise
recruits for the cavalry branch of the Contingent to
any extent. Was it likely then that a man so well-
known, living within thirty miles of Delhi, in an
important town not a stone of which had been
touched—whose inhabitants instead of flocking to
welcome our approach, hid like toads in their holes,
—was it likely, I ask, that this man had been living
an immaculate life devoted to our service? Was it
in the order of things that he could have remained
neutral? No one but men tainted with the weakest

of political opinions which prevailed in the North West, would have dreamt of such a thing.

Had the column been accompanied, for political purposes, by a civilian of the Punjaub stamp—men who, taking their cue from Sir John Lawrence, indulge in a little common sense, and possess the feelings of soldiers as well as collectors of revenue—or even had Colonel Greathed been left to his own judgment, the advance of the column would have been of more essential service to the State, and punishment would have been administered where it was merited. Will it be believed? as we entered Koorjah, a skeleton was stuck up on the roadside, exposed to public gaze, against a wall. The head had been severed from the body, and cuts in the shin bones were apparent, inflicted by some sharp instrument; and in the opinion of a medical committee, this skeleton was that of a European female. But still the town paid a large sum yearly to Government, and on that account, in the opinion of the collector, was to be spared.

But the history given of the skeleton by " our faithful Mahomedan pensioner," showed, that after finding himself at large and unscathed, he considered any amount of humbug would pass current. His account was that " the skeleton was that of an old man who had died from hunger some time ago, and his body had not been removed!"

Was anything more absurd? Did any one ever hear of a Mahomedan or Hindoo corpse being allowed to rot in the streets of a town; and that, apparently, a well-regulated one? But before many hours had passed, a still small rumour flew through the camp that the town was not wholly filled with innocents; and towards evening it was well known that a number of armed men had barricaded themselves in their houses, and civilly declined to give up their arms. Mark the consequences!

Colonel Greathed was well aware that a number of rebels of all sorts—butchers, bakers, men let loose from the gaol, others who had fled from Delhi, in fact, a miscellaneous armed mob—were awaiting our arrival at Allyghur, distant only about thirty miles; and that the Bareilly Brigade, commanded by the subadar Bukht Khan, who had raised the standard of rebellion at Bareilly, had crossed the Jumna at Muttra, and would try to form a junction with them, in order to seize the Fort of Allyghur, a most important position on the Grand Trunk Road. To send a force into a strange town at night was madness, while it was equally impossible to make any delay and thus risk the loss of Allyghur.

The men who in the morning, armed as loyal police, had sallied forth to meet the collector, had not the power to disarm the rebels in Koorjah; the consequence was that they remained with their arms: the column marched on to Allyghur, and the collector bolted back at full speed to Bolundshur, where the Belooch Battalion, with a couple of guns, were left for the protection of the station. So much for immaculate Koorjah!

Two marches brought us to Allyghur, where, as before stated, we had heard that a number of villains were prepared to resist the advance of the column, believing that it was only a small detachment sent out from Agra; this opinion was strengthened by the advanced guard, composed only of a small detachment of cavalry, falling back (when fired into) upon the main column.

Out came the villains, yelling like a set of infuriated demon; but their Io Pœans were of short duration. Major Turner, with H. M.'s 75th, the 4th Punjaub Infantry, and some guns, passed round to the right. Captain Blunt immediately came into action, and silenced the fire of a brass gun and several "telegraph guns,"* which were placed in breastworks across the

---

* Guns made out of the sockets of the telegraph posts; a most ingenious but not very safe arrangement.

road, and at the various gates of the city. Major
Ouvry, with the cavalry and No. 17 Battery, took
a cast to the left towards the cantonments; passing
in skirmishing order through the various compounds
and gardens, which were chiefly deserted.

After a long detour of about four miles, the two
columns met on the opposite side of the town. Like
a babbling pack who in heavy cover has lost all
scent of reynard, each inquired what had become
of the enemy; who, at the first discovery of the grief
into which they had fallen, made off at once.

Not a soul in the town seemed inclined to give
any information as to their whereabouts, until an old
woman, possessing as little the powers of taciturnity
as the rest of her sex, let out that their Penates
having been sent on ahead, they had taken the route
to Akbarabad, hoping there to fall in with the
Bareilly Brigade under Bukht Khan.

Major Ouvry, by whom a chase after Pandy was
not to be resisted, started at once, and after a three
miles' trot, we came upon the whole detachment;
which, including women and children, amounted to
some 500 persons, with thirty or forty carts of house-
hold stuff.

The fair riders, with the utmost politeness, were
requested to descend, and after an inquisitorial search

into the contents of the carts, were allowed to depart. While domestic arrangements were thus being carried on by some of the less active of the party, Major Ouvry had made his dispositions for " a bag."

Unlike a true member of the chase, who loves to see his fox take well to the open, he had headed his game; spreading his cavalry right and left of the road, to beat back the high crops with which the country was covered, and into which the enemy had skulked.

Forming his line precisely as he would have beaten a field of turnips for game, a scene commenced which baffles all description; pea-fowl, partridges, and Pandies rose together: the latter gave the best sport. Here might be seen a Lancer running a-tilt at a wretch who unfortunately had taken to the open; there a Punjaub trooper cutting right and left as his victims rose before him; while the enemy, who were Goojahs and armed with swords and hatchets, started up as the line approached, and dashed at their nearest opponent.

Two troopers and a horse were our only casualties, while about 100 brace of Goojahs bit the dust. A detachment of the column was left at Allyghur to garrison the fort.

At Akbarabad, our next march, resided two brothers, Mungal and Mytab Sing, Rajpoot chiefs; who, during the mutiny, had made themselves conspicuous by their rebellious conduct. The cavalry arrived there at daylight, and surrounded the town; and the two brothers were caught and slain as they were attempting to make their escape. Three guns were found in the town loaded and primed, but such was the surprise, that they had not even had time to fire them. A large quantity of powder and ammunition was secreted in the palace, which was blown up, and the city burnt to the ground. The few inhabitants that were caught were summarily executed; and the bodies of the two chiefs were hung to the boughs of the trees outside, on the public road.

The 8th of October was devoted to a halt; on the 9th the column marched, by a cross road, to Brijghur, a very pretty fortified position, in most flourishing case. Far distant from the great arterial thoroughfares, it had in no way been molested by the mutineers; and an indigo factory, a short distance from the town, had been preserved from destruction. Even the hens, which in these troublous times had refused elsewhere to supply our breakfast-table, here had conducted their domestic duties in the ordinary routine, and by their cackling welcomed our advent as their best of friends.

At this distance even from Agra, loud croakings were heard: epistles imploring aid, in every language both dead and living, and in cypher, forwarded by Government special messengers, and received by Colonel Greathed, came pouring into camp. Many, like the dreams of Pharaoh, were beyond the interpretation of the soothsayers, and no Joseph was at hand. All, however, that could be made out of the business was, that the people at Agra were in a cruel stew about some enemy supposed to be hovering round the neighbourhood with a siege train. The Cavalry and Horse Artillery, it was insisted, must go on at once; and as Colonel Greathed felt that he had come within the clutches of the hydra-headed powers of the North-Western Government, they were despatched on the 8th, at midnight, with instructions to push on rapidly to Agra, a distance of forty-eight miles. The infantry and the field battery followed four hours afterwards, arriving early in the morning at Hattrass, a well-built town, in an apparently flourishing condition, through which Bukht Khan's force had marched a few days previously, levying a heavy fine for its ransom.

[8]   H

As we got nearer to Agra, the plot was getting hotter and hotter. Despatches, more and more urgent, were received by Colonel Greathed. "His credit would be at stake if Agra was attacked, and he so near: they were threatened, and in momentary dread of an attack; in fact, we must push on to the utmost, for if we delayed, we should only find their ghosts to reproach us for their murder."

A few hours only were given us to rest the cattle at Hattrass. The European infantry were carried on elephants, carts, and camels, and all were pushed on to overtake the cavalry and horse artillery. This being effected, we crossed the Jumna in one body at the bridge of boats, at sunrise on the morning of the 10th, to relieve the garrison of a fort possessing an inexhaustible supply of ordnance and ammunition, amply supplied with provisions, and capable, from its strength, of defying the whole army of Pandies for an indefinite time.

CHAPTER IX.

AGRA.

LITTLE did the appearance of Agra give token of the terrible emergency which required that an army, whose infantry, from prior exposure and service, were far from being in good health, should march forty-four miles, with but a few hours' rest, to its succour.

The 3rd Bengal European regiment, neatly dressed, sleek and well favoured compared with the battered state of our regiments, was mounted on the bastion, and cheered us heartily as the force passed under the walls of the citadel.

Ladies were riding and driving about in all directions; yeomanry cavalry were careering in full equestrian pride, while from every hole and corner loomed the ugly muzzle of an iron monster, ready to annihilate any amount of Pandies.

The fort itself, large and well built, was in perfect repair; and with its high double walls and deep ditch, would have been reduced with difficulty, even by a

European force. The appearance outside, however, was deceptive; the holiday-makers were the
exceptions, not the rule of the place; and the ladies
represented certainly the most cheerful portion of the
community. We were kept grilling on the public
roads for two hours, while the local executives
argued with Colonel Greathed as to whether it
would not be more advisable to encamp the column
in a series of gardens overgrown with brushwood,
where the guns would not have had a range of fifty
yards, and where the cavalry could not possibly act,
in preference to a magnificent grassy plain, with
not an obstacle within three or four hundred yards
of our front, and those only a few high crops.

Fortunate indeed was it that Colonel Greathed's
better judgment prevailed, as the sequel will show.

It was finally arranged that the force should
encamp on the Native Infantry parade. No sooner
was the camp marked out, and the horses picquetted,
than it was crowded with men of all descriptions
from the fort. To our great disappointment, we
were positively informed, that hearing of our
approach, the enemy had again retired beyond the
Karee Nuddee, a stream about nine miles distant.

The baggage was just arriving, there were but few
tents up, the Artillerymen had obtained permission

to lie down in a house hard by, and many officers had gone to see their friends in Agra. All were much knocked up, and in a few minutes most were in the arms of Morpheus; but in a very short time we were all roused to the conviction that something was wrong. This was confirmed by a round shot coming through the mess-tent; and as I rushed out at one door of my tent, a servant was bowled down at the other by a second round shot. All were instantly on the alert: the conduct of our troops was beyond praise ; that stern discipline which war alone teaches, stood us in good stead. A shower of round shot from a battery of twelve guns on our right and front, came dashing into camp, spreading terror among the camp-followers, and still greater alarm to the sightseers.

Such was the terrible panic among the latter, that those officers who had gone into the Fort, and were eager to get back to their posts, could not stem the torrent of affrighted beings: an officer of the Dragoons in attempting it, was fairly carried off his legs and borne back with the crowd. Not satisfied with legitimate means of escape, the gun horses in many cases were seized as they were being led to the guns, and were found next morning in the Fort.

In the mean time the troops had not been idle. The artillerymen, having no time to think of their accoutrements, rushed to their guns, and from the park opened such a fire upon the enemy's position, as led them to see that they had found their match. The horses were soon put to, the cavalry in their saddles, and the infantry awaiting orders on parade.

It was evident that the sooner an advance was made the better. Camp-followers and horses were falling fast in camp, and the native grooms, panic stricken, loosed from their picquets many horses, which were gallopping about in all directions. The distance of the park from the enemy's position was too great to hope to silence their guns, which were of heavy metal. Captain Remmington's troop, supported by a portion of the infantry and Punjaub Cavalry, was directed to advance on the right; three guns of No. 17 Battery, being of heavier metal than the Horse Artillery guns, were left to cover the advance from the centre, supported by the guard left for the protection of the camp; while the remainder of the battery, with Captain Blunt's troop, supported by H.M.'s 9th Lancers *, and detachments of H.M.'s 75th Foot and 2nd Punjaub Infantry,† advanced

---

* A species of freemasonry existed between the 9th Lancers and Artillery: at the first whisper of a brush a squadron attached itself at once to each battery as its support; at last it became quite a habit to look out for it before attempting a move.

† These gallant fellows had marched already on foot forty-four miles in the previous thirty hours.

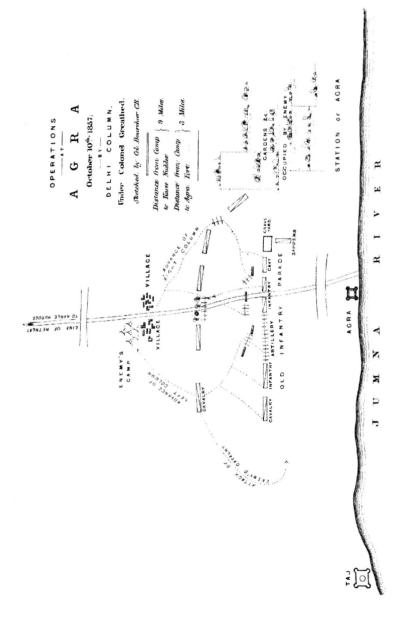

OPERATIONS
AT
A G R A
October 10th. 1857.
— BY —
DELHI COLUMN.
Under Colonel Greathed.
Sketched by Col. Bourchier CB.

Distance from Camp
to Kare Nuddee   } 9 Miles.
Distance from Camp
to Agra Fort.   } 3 Miles.

TO KARKE NUDDEE
LINE OF RETREAT

VILLAGE

VILLAGE

ENEMY'S CAMP

ADVANCE OF RIGHT COLUMN

ADVANCE OF LEFT COLUMN

ATTACK BY ENEMY'S CAVALRY

CAVALRY

CAVALRY

INFANTRY

INFANTRY

ARTILLERY

CAV.

CAV.

INFANTRY

OLD INFANTRY PARADE

GRAVE YARD

SAPPERS

GARDENS &c.

OCCUPIED BY ENEMY

STATION OF AGRA

AGRA

TAJ

J U M N A   R I V E R

from the left towards a mosque, round which the greater portion of the enemy's guns were posted. The Agra Battery and the 3rd Europeans subsequently joined on the right; the column being thus formed into two divisions. The infantry were soon busily at work, dislodging the enemy from the gardens in which it had been suggested that we should encamp; and which were even then in the hands of the enemy.

A large body of cavalry was completely routed by the Punjaub Cavalry in gallant style, under their leaders, Captains Probyn, Watson, and Younghusband, three guns being captured in the charge; while the fire of the remainder of the enemy's artillery was sensibly diminished. The practice of Captain Remmington's troop was particularly effective: three ammunition waggons were exploded by his shot.

On the left, however, a large body of cavalry which had been for some time observed hovering about, made a dash into camp. Captain Blunt, with his guns and a squadron of Lancers, fell back as a reinforcement to the guard left for its protection, meeting the cavalry as they came in; a splendid charge from the Lancers, in which unfortunately Captain French was killed and Lieutenant Jones dangerously wounded, dispersed the enemy's cavalry as a body, and eventually (but not until they had executed a large amount of mischief) they were driven from the camp or destroyed in it.

Steadily our whole force advanced, supported by the infantry, until the enemy's fire was entirely silenced and the position near the mosque, with several guns, captured.

It being evident that the enemy were in full retreat towards the Karee Nuddee, a pursuit by the artillery and cavalry was immediately ordered.

About four miles on the Gwalior road, sheltered by two villages, was the camp of the enemy. Apparently, both divisions of our force came within sight of it at the same time, and arrived at the same moment. Forming line, we together flew through its streets, driving the enemy before us.

Only once did they again make a stand; a few rounds of grape, however, scattered them in all directions, and the cavalry were soon among their flying ranks, doing great execution. For seven miles the road was one continued line of carts, guns, ammunition waggons, camels rushing about without their drivers, and baggage of every description; all of which fell into our hands. Not a gun or cart recrossed the stream; all became a prize, owing to the rapidity with which the victory was followed up on the opposite bank : a few cavalry troopers made their appearance, but soon disappeared, after a few rounds from the Horse Artillery. Thirteen pieces of ordnance, with an enormous quantity of ammunition, were brought into camp; much that was useless was destroyed, and the enemy's camp, with the villages on which it abutted, were burnt.

Seven of the captured guns were of native manufacture, and in many parts covered with Persian and Hindoo inscriptions. Three were of enormous weight, though only eighteen and 12-pounders : these had been brought from Dhalpoor, for the purpose, doubtless, of attempting to breach the walls of Agra; but they had not a mortar with them.

The force returned to camp at about 7 o'clock, having marched sixty-six miles, and fought a general action in thirty-nine hours : nine miles of the route had been done by the cavalry and artillery, at a trot, through high crops and ploughed fields.

Truly we had reason to be thankful to Providence for the successful issue of our day's work; which at first looked far from promising. As it turned out, nothing could have been more successful, or better managed; but the culpable ignorance of the Agra authorities—who summoned a force to their rescue from a distance, and on its arrival allowed it to be led into an ambuscade, by repeated assurances, up to within half an hour of the attack, that the enemy had retired beyond the Karee Nuddee—seems hardly credible. It could have been no sudden thought of the enemy, or the work of a moment, to have brought their guns such a distance, and crossed them over a river with a stream scarcely fordable, flowing over a bed of deep sand: it must have been the work of many days, and of unremitting labour. The presence of the enemy's camp within four miles of the fort, and their possession of the actual ground on which the Agra authorities wished us to encamp, shows how painfully little the latter were aware of what was passing so close to them.

That the surprise was mutual there can be no doubt. The enemy believed that the reported arrival of a column from Delhi was only an imposition, and hung the spy by whom our arrival was chronicled: they imagined that the Agra force had crossed the river during the night, and marched back again in the morning. The small number of tents pitched, and the little show the camp made, strengthened this belief, and led to the attack upon our position.

For political reasons, it was said, the town of Agra was spared: no fine, even, was levied upon it; although it was well known that the inhabitants were cognisant of the presence of the enemy, whose camp had been supplied with provisions and sweetmeats from the city.

Scenes the most ludicrous passed before our eyes as we returned to camp. First, came a fat old gentleman, on as fat an old horse, who requested Major Ouvry to give him a certificate to the effect that he had been under fire, he being the commandant of some volunteers of whose whereabouts he was in total ignorance; next came a truly perspiring hero, jogging along with his bridle and drawn sword in one hand, while in the other was a fan of enormous size, which he managed with dexterous address; while further on might be seen a corpulent clerk, brandishing his stick over a fallen Pandy, ever and anon starting at his own temerity.

David wisely says, " It is good for me that I have been in trouble," but it is doubtful whether the benefit extends to Englishmen incarcerated in a fortress, be it even as strong as Agra; certain it is that affairs were in a most gloomy state within its walls, and to those who had been at Delhi at the very worst of times, it seemed incomprehensible. The real state of the country now was comparatively *couleur de rose*, but the black clouds of despair seemed to have settled down at Agra like a pall. So different too from the Punjaub,* where all were, even at the worst, hopeful; here it was continually instilled into our minds that the worst was not yet come; that Gwalior and Lucknow had still to be subdued, and that although Delhi might have fallen, &c., &c.: in short, we were in a bad way.

The ladies, poor creatures, were most to be pitied; several said that night after night they had to listen to the croakers indulging in wonder as to whether in the morning any of them would be alive, and would gladly, had it been permitted, have risked the dangers of a march with us to Cawnpore, to have escaped from their present imprisonment.

Our men and cattle being much in want of rest, the 11th, 12th, and 13th October were halts. The ammunition was filled up from the Fort, and our two 5½-inch mortars were exchanged for two 8-inch. The wounded were sent into the hospital which had been established in the Mootee Musjid, where they were attended not only by the medical officers, but by the ladies; many of whom visited the wards daily,

---

* An officer of the civil service, who had been translated to the North-Western Provinces (at the time a perfect stranger to me), caught me by the hand, and begged I would come into his hut and talk to him of the Punjaub, as it did his heart good to hear of the doings there.

administering little comforts to the sick and dying. It was indeed a touching sight to see our fair country-women, many of whom were themselves bowed down by affliction, seated by the bedside of the wounded soldier. "They will in no wise lose their reward."

Of course we all visited the Taj, which has been so often described, that the less now said about it the better; it is certainly very beautiful: in fact the most beautiful building in India. Many ladies flying from the gloomy captivity of the Fort, made it an excuse for a morning's holiday, fluttering about in all the weakness of "the last new muslin," and seeming to enjoy themselves like larks escaped from a cage.

To see their happiness was ample reward for the fatigue we had undergone on their behalf.

CHAPTER X.

EVENTS AT CAWNPORE.

EARLY on the morning of the 14th October, the column crept stealthily out of Agra; doubtful, indeed, how far we should get away, ere, local timidity being excited, we should be recalled from the more urgent duty—the relief of the Lucknow Garrison. Havelock, it was true, had forced his entrance into the Residency; but he was himself there besieged, and all were clamorous to get on as fast as possible.

The first march was to the Rambagh, where we were reinforced by two siege guns, and detachments of H. M.'s 8th and 75th regiments. Many of the ladies and officers were tempted to come out thus far, the result being a most delightful pic-nic in the gardens.

The 15th brought the column to a ruined tomb called Boorya-ka-Talao (the old woman's tank), and without much incident arrived on the 19th at Myn-poorie, a civil station.

General Grant had arrived, and assumed command on the 16th at Ferozabad.

The Rajah of Mynpoorie had, early in the mutiny, thrown off the British allegiance; but most of the officers attached to the troops at the station, as also the civilians, had escaped to Agra.

Prior, however, to his departure, Mr. Power the collector had entrusted the balance of Government treasure, amounting to between 20,000*l.* and 30,000*l.* to the care of a relative of the Rajah's; and it was deposited in the Fort.

It was said that the Rajah, who had guns and a large body of armed retainers, with some companies of sepoys, would make a stand in the Fort.

Within a few miles of the city the aforesaid relative, commonly called the Rao, attended only by three or four unarmed followers, came out to make his obeisance; informing the General that the Rajah was still in his fort, where (being generally in a state of intoxication) we might hope to make him a prisoner. The column arrived at Mynpoorie on the 19th October at about noon, after a hot and dusty march of twenty-four miles; but the Rajah had beat a retreat at midnight.

The city was uninjured; but the civil station was a mass of ruins; and the church, gaol, court-houses, in fact, everything resembling the residence of a European, were destroyed.

A party was immediately sent to take military possession of the Fort, while Mr. Power proceeded on what he feared was a hopeless errand, to search for his treasure. The Fort was deserted, but the owner had evidently gone off in a hurry; as the guns were left loaded, in position, and strange to say, the treasure was found exactly where Mr. Power had deposited it, and "in full tale."

It is difficult to conceive under what circumstances so large a sum had been saved. The Rao himself may have been able to resist the temptation with a view to future benefits; but how its existence was kept a secret from the Rajah (who, as an acknowledged traitor, could expect no favour from the British Government under any circumstances) is indeed a mystery: or if its existence was known to the Rajah, why was it not appropriated or carried off, when he left the previous night? That might easily have been done, he having a number of elephants and carriages with him.

The bags of coin were deposited in a little room with a slight door of open railings. However, there it was, and proved a most acceptable addition to the Commissariat treasure-chest.

The Fort was not, as before stated, entirely deserted: as the gates were opened, we found that a snow-white army, headed by a commander in black with a red helmet, formed the garrison; or, to drop allegory, a flock of geese, headed by a magnificent turkey in all the pride of fantail and scarlet top-knot, cackled forth a hearty welcome. Traitors all, like their masters, a summary sentence of death was passed, and immediately carried out; every man carried off his prize, and a glorious feast was the result.

In addition to private property of every kind and description, an enormous quantity of powder was discovered under the fort; several very well cast guns were in different stages of manufacture, while others were on the lathes: one, lately finished, was found in a well; and a large quantity of ammunition was stored in the fort. But the occupation and final destruction of the fort by the military authorities was not carried out without immense opposition on the part of the Commissioner; though the prize agent had been sent to seize the whole of the property of the Rajah, which was confiscated. The Rao begged and implored that one portion might not be touched, it being his own private property and that of his daughter: he vowed and declared that not a stitch belonging either to Government or to any European was concealed there. The Commissioner, believing him, by turns protested, entreated, and implored that the warbrobe might not be touched; in fact, the Government could not be carried on if it was, &c., &c. Fortunately, in this case, the house was divided against itself: Mr. Power having lost his all at Mynpoorie, shrewdly guessed that a few odds and ends of his own might turn up, and had not such implicit faith in the word of a native.*

By way of compromise, it was agreed that the doors should be opened, and we should cursorily inspect the interior. The first object that came to view was a huge Government drum; the second (Power's face of delight was worth coming the distance to see) was a box: not, as will be supposed, containing the gorgeous turban and velvet chupkin,† of the Rao, or the skeleton petticoat and dainty slippers of his daughter, but a most unexceptionable array of coats and inexpressibles, Power's lost property. This, to a man who on the whole liked a neat turn-out,

---

* The word of a native, except when it suits his own interests, is never to be believed. "As soon as they are born they go about telling lies." In the "Prem Sagur," a purely Hindoo work, a dancing girl thus addresses Khrishna, who appears before her as an humble bee, with black velvety coat and sharp sting:

"Ham jante hein jetna siyàm badan hein etna Sab Kapatihein."

Everything that has a black body is deceitful.

† Coat worn by a Mussulman.

and had been condemned for months to one single shooting-coat, was a glorious find. Nothing more was said of the immaculate Rao, and the whole fort was made over to the tender mercies of the prize agent and engineer.* Each well performed his duties; the prize was sold by auction, and the fort was destroyed.

On the morning of the 21st of October, the column left Mynpoorie for Bewar, the junction of the four roads leading to Cawnpore, Meerut, Futtehghur, and Agra.

Reports were afloat that we should find the position defended by wonderfully strong batteries and innumerable guns. All proved matters of fiction. A picquet, detached from Futtehghur, fell back at our approach, and, unmolested, the camp was established. General Grant's orders from Agra were to steer clear of Futtehghur, which we were all itching to be at. It was doubtless, however, a wise measure not to molest the hornets' nest until we were

---

* A most ludicrous occurrence took place. The prize agent was surrounded by an *embarras de richesse*, which he could find nobody to load on the carts. A man of the 9th Lancers, who with upturned sleeves had been working very hard, saw the Rao standing idle, and not knowing who it was, all darkies being alike in his eyes, caught him by the back of the neck and pushed him on with a " Sure, and why shouldn't you carry a load as well as me, you big black thief."

fully prepared to occupy the fort; as to have taken it and again given it up would only have insured the destruction of the whole stock of timber of the gun carriage agency, with its steam and other valuable machinery, and the whole clothing of the army in the North-West, which was stored in that station.

From natives travelling along the road we learnt that an engagement had been a few days previously fought about ten miles from Cawnpore; that the enemy had been routed, but that being utterly without cavalry, the General had not been able to follow up his advantage, and that the guns were still lurking about in the neighbourhood of Kanooj.

On the morning of the 23rd, on arriving at Meerunka Serai, near Kanooj, the Quartermaster-General with his guard, while reconnoitring close to the town situated on the banks of a stream, was fired upon from a battery on the opposite side, supported by about 500 infantry, all hard at work trying to get the guns across the river. The report of the firing made General Grant at once send down two horse artillery guns and a squadron of dragoons to the scene of action. Lieutenant Murray, who commanded, took the bull by the horns; at a gallop he went close to the banks of the river, forming battery at the water's edge, and soon silenced his opponents on the opposite bank. The infantry fled, pursued by the dragoons and some Punjaub cavalry. Nearly the whole detachment was cut up; about six only escaping to the Ganges. Four guns, with a large quantity of ammunition, were brought into camp, together with a number of large draft bullocks.

On the 26th, after four ordinary marches, we arrived at Cawnpore, then the centre of the mutinous districts.

To any one who had lived at Cawnpore in its sunny days, its present appearance was a most distressing commentary upon the events which had there occurred within the last six months. It was a perfect wreck; few houses were standing, and both the churches had been destroyed and defiled. At one time the largest station in India, now scarcely a stone was left upon another. The Assembly Rooms, Theatre, and Masonic Lodge, with two or three houses not of an inflammable nature, or which were the property of natives, were all that remained.

But if these were sad tokens of the destruction of property, Wheeler's entrenchment, and the massacre-house, told tales of blood too frightful even to think upon.

It will be remembered that, at the time of the outbreak, General Wheeler had a very small detach-

ment of Europeans in the garrison of Cawnpore,
two companies of H. M.'s 84th arrived in the beginning of June, one of which, with a company of the
32nd, was despatched to Sir Henry Lawrence at
Lucknow, leaving General Wheeler with only

> 60 men H. M.'s 84th.
> 70 men H. M.'s 32nd.
> 59 men Bengal Artillery.
> 15 men 1st Bengal Fusiliers.
>
> Total—204

with six field guns. The native force consisted of
three regiments of infantry, one of Regular and one
of Irregular Cavalry, and three guns of an Oude
battery; which, at the time *en route* to Futtehghur,
was halted at Cawnpore: in all about 4,000 men,
with three guns, the whole of the magazine, and inexhaustible stores of ammunition at their disposal.

In addition to the details already given above,
General Wheeler had to provide for the safety of a
large party of merchants, pensioners, railway and
canal officials, with their families; besides all the
ladies and children of the officers at the station, and
of the troops at Lucknow.

The odds against him were frightful; his game a
most desperate one.

The Nana, a Mahratta of wealth and influence,
resided in his fort at Bithoor, about twelve miles

from Cawnpore. His general intelligence, his love
of European society, and above all the fact of his
welfare apparently depending on the prosperity of
British rule, made it most probable that, of all men,
he would most tenaciously stick by us.

His aid was solicited in the crisis, and cheerfully
given. The Government Treasury was made over
to his charge and guarded by his troops. But the
true Mahratta thirst for blood was only lying dor-
mant: he was ready, when the time came, to make
his deadly spring. It was not till the beginning
of June that the native troops of Cawnpore showed
signs of disaffection.

The warnings given at Delhi and Meerut had not
been disregarded, and by the 4th of June an entrenchment, provided with food for twenty-five days, was
finished; into which the whole European population
was moved. On the morning of the 6th, the cavalry,
who at nearly every station showed the first and
bitterest feelings of mutiny, rose; they were followed
by the regiments of the line and the gunners of
the Oude Battery. The Nana, who still held the
treasury, sent word that he meant to attack the
entrenchment.

For twenty days the devoted band of Europeans
held out against one continued attack from all sides.

Night and day, twelve pieces of ordnance were playing upon the position, in perfect security, their gunners being sheltered by the large buildings by which it was surrounded. The appearance of the frightfully-shattered buildings told its fearful tale. Every shot seemed to have told upon the walls, while those from the heavier pieces went through and through the buildings, carrying death and destruction in their path : not a square yard of the walls seemed to have escaped.

This precarious shelter was not long allowed to these poor sufferers. The roofs were soon ignited by the bursting shells, and nothing then remained to shelter them from the burning rays of a June's noonday sun. There were two wells ; but one alone supplied them with water, and to approach it in the day time was all but certain death, it being completely commanded by musketry ; the other had been appropriated as a sepulchre of the dead. Notwithstanding their overpowering numbers, these cowards never once dared to attempt to storm the entrenchment, although the defences were merely nominal ; feeling sure that starvation must eventually lead the defenders to capitulate. Was it then to be wondered at that General Wheeler, whose position was hopeless on the 25th of June, should have listened to the pro-

mise of the Nana that the garrison should receive
a safe passage to Allahabad, excepting such as were
connected with the government of Lord Dalhousie.*

The terms were agreed to, and officers were sent on
the 26th to see the boats, which were found com-
modious and well appointed; carts were sent for the
sick, and hopes rose of a speedy deliverance from
their bondage: during which it might with truth be
said "the iron had entered into their souls."

On the 27th the survivors were put on board the
boats provided by the Nana; when an act of treachery
commenced more cowardly and diabolical than history
had ever recorded. Guns were unmasked as if by
magic, and musketry poured in withering volleys
from all sides. The boats which had been loosed from
their moorings drifted ashore, and the women and
children who had had the misfortune to survive the
second massacre, were dragged to a small house in
the station, which was their tomb.

These scenes had passed away; but the shattered

* The bitter spirit shown by the Nana against Lord Dalhousie's
government was caused by the discontinuance of the pension
granted to the late Peishwah Bajee Rao; who having no sons, had
adopted the Nana, and declared to the British Government that
he was to succeed him. A second cause was the conversion
of a 5 into a 4 per cent. loan, by Lord Dalhousie; in the former
the Nana was a great holder of stock, and consequently a heavy
loser.

walls told their tale of woe. Wandering about the intrenchment, British soldiers of every rank might be seen searching for little mementoes of their fallen countrymen so foully murdered. Revenge deep and bitter was vowed against the perpetrators of such atrocities. I confess to have been no stranger to the influence exercised on the mind by these scenes: the very worst feelings rose to the surface. Here might be seen a dragoon with a child's frock on the end of his lance, on which he had vowed never to spare a sepoy; there a soldier with a fair tress attached to his bayonet, determined on future revenge.

Could it be wondered at? Twice I passed the ruins, and the same feelings on both occasions seemed to rise involuntarily. I resolved never again to enter its precincts, and although on a subsequent occasion my tent abutted for six days on a corner of the intrenchment, I religiously kept my word.

The fatal well, the grave of so many of that band of heroes, was carefully covered in. Who could pass it unmoved? If the intrenchment was horrible, the massacre house was infinitely more so: in the inner court-yard was a tree on which were traces of the murder of the poor little innocents, whose hair, sticking to the bark, told of the dreadful death they had met.

On the day of General Havelock's victory at Cawnpore, the 16th of July, the whole of the survivors were murdered. They had been imprisoned since the 27th of the preceding month, and treated with the greatest rigour. The rooms were riddled with musket-bullets; the floor saturated with blood; while here and there were sentences scratched upon the walls, descriptive of their sufferings, and calling on their countrymen to inflict severe retribution.

The bodies had been buried near the spot in a well, over which a neat tomb had been erected by a detachment of H. M.'s 32nd Regiment.

To record more of such scenes of horror would be of little use. The soldiers needed no hounding on to excite them to revenge: the difficulty was to prevent them from considering everyone with a black face as an enemy.

Orders having been received from Sir Colin Campbell, the column, reinforced by several detachments, was directed to prepare to cross the Ganges into Oude.

CHAPTER XI.

THE RELIEF OF LUCKNOW.

THE relief of the garrison of Lucknow forms another act in the tragedy of 1857. General Inglis in his despatches has so touchingly told the tale, that it is only necessary here to state that early in June the native troops in the cantonments of Oude mutinied. The late lamented Sir Henry Lawrence then made immediate preparations for the defence of the Residency; which, providentially, he was enabled partially to effect, as no attack was threatened until the 29th of June. From that date the Lucknow garrison, although augmented by the gallant force under General Havelock, was in a state of the strictest siege until the 17th of November, when the force under Sir Colin Campbell opened communications with the Residency.

It does not come within the limits of this narrative to enter upon the various circumstances which rendered the endurance and fortitude of the garrison so remarkable.

The death of Sir Henry Lawrence cannot be passed over in silence by one who was so deeply indebted to him.* As a public servant it would be superfluous, if not presumptuous, to say a word even in his praise: all felt that his loss was a national one; and no man was more deeply imbued with the greatest of Christian graces. To benefit mankind was his heart's delight; but the classes whose condition he chiefly aimed to ameliorate were the wives and children of the soldiers. The Lawrence Asylums at Sonawar and Mount Aboo are noble and lasting monuments to his memory.

But to return to our narrative. The column crossed the Ganges on the 30th of October, passing on the opposite bank the remains of several batteries which had been opposed to General Havelock's advance, and encamping on the 1st of November near a stream at Bunnee, crossed by a ford; the bridge having been destroyed by the rebels.

On the 2nd the camp was moved a short distance, to Banterah; and it became evident that although hitherto unmolested, we must hope for no stores or

---

* In 1848, I was anxious to be appointed to do duty at the Warley Depot for recruits; and knowing nobody at the India House, I asked Sir Henry Lawrence for his interest. Before replying to my letter, he immediately went to town, asked for, and obtained for me the appointment I was so anxious to hold.

assistance of any kind from the villages; each of which was the home of our enemies, the great majority of the sepoy army having been drawn from Oude: in fact, every village was in arms.

While marking out the camp, Captain Roberts, of the Artillery, who was officiating as Quartermaster-General of the force, was, with his little party, attacked by infantry and cavalry from a village hard by, narrowly escaping with their lives. An immediate attack was made upon this village; and two others, which fired upon the approaching column, were carried and destroyed, though not without opposition. Major Ouvry, with a party of cavalry, was nearly surrounded, and had to send back for reinforcements; but he eventually extricated himself from his position.

A running fight was kept up for some hours; a brass 9-pounder gun was captured in a village, and the enemy, who had apparently come out from Lucknow to see what we were made of, retired into the city.

Nothing particular occurred on the 3rd and 4th; but on the 5th, No. 17 Battery was ordered to form part of a large convoy, which was to escort an enormous string of camels and carts loaded with ammunition and corn to the Alumbagh, where the depôt for the relieving and relieved army was to be formed.

It may be well here to mention that this position had been held and fortified by a body of our troops, with light and heavy artillery, from the time that General Havelock forced his way into Lucknow, on the 25th of September. The post was a most important one, not only as a fortified depôt, but as a chain in the link of communications, which it was necessary now to keep open, between Lucknow and Cawnpore.

We arrived at a grove of trees within half a mile of the Bagh without molestation, and it was determined that we should halt there for a day, while the stores were being deposited in safety.

Towards mid-day, a body of cavalry menaced our flanks, and some light guns opened upon our right; but a few rounds from our artillery, and a gallant charge of cavalry, scattered the enemy.

A more serious engagement, followed by the entire defeat of the portion of our force engaged, took place later in the afternoon.

To secure our flanks, some companies of the 93rd Highlanders, two guns, and a troop of Lancers, had been posted at a village fronting the Fort of Jellalabad, at that time held by the enemy in force.

All things seemed quiet; and, having been ordered to procure a return of the ordnance and ordnance stores in the depôt, and to get some idea of the nature of the surrounding country and of the enemy's batteries, I galloped off, and from the top of a large house inside the enclosure, witnessed, with several others, what appeared to be a dire disaster.

From the direction of the advanced picquet alluded to, a cloud of dust at first was seen, then a few horsemen and loose horses, after them the troop of dragoons and my two guns, and last of all the Highlanders, running towards the main body of the convoy in the maddest confusion; yet no enemy was in view, and no firing was heard: still that the detachment was flying from some imminent danger there was no doubt, and with our glasses we could see the remainder of the party getting under arms. Not a moment was to be lost; and a few minutes brought us to the scene of action. There a scene the most ridiculous conceivable was being enacted: peal after peal of uncontrollable laughter greeted us, as with anxious faces we rode into the bivouac; and it was some time ere we could discover what was the cause of the apparent disaster and subsequent mirth.

It appears that, while idly dosing on the ground,

two officers espied in a tree an immense bees-nest.
Possessed by the demon of mischief, they commenced
pelting it with clods; and this not answering their
purpose, a lance was thrown, with deadly aim, into
the centre of it.

The disgraceful flight we had witnessed was
now easily accounted for; one of the perpetrators
of the mischief was dangerously ill from the effects;
but, as a body, the kilted Highlanders suffered most,
and they bolted, taking with them more bees than they
carried in their bonnets. The result proved the truth
of the old adage, that "idleness is the root of all
evil." The convoy, without further adventure,
returned late at night to camp.

On the 9th October, Sir Colin Campbell, after a
ride of nearly forty miles, joined the camp; and on
the 11th he reviewed the whole force, which day by
day had been increased by detachments of all arms.

On the morning of the 12th, the whole force
marched towards the Alumbagh. No sooner had the
head of the column arrived at the road leading to
the Fort of Jellalabad, than a fire was opened from
some light guns, which had been placed in a line of
field works.

The artillery and cavalry were quickly formed in
front; the field works were soon evacuated, and two

[8]   K

guns of small calibre captured, in a gallant charge of the Punjaub Cavalry, under Lieutenant Gough.

On the morning of the 13th, a brigade was formed under Brigadier Hope to take possession of Jellalabad, which had been evacuated. The fort, a strong one of thick mud, with good flanking defences, was empty. A breach having been made in it by mining, one side was blown in, and the troops were withdrawn.

The camp was formed on the Cawnpore side of the Alumbagh, but being under fire of some heavy guns in battery near the canal, it was retired some little distance out of their range. The whole of the camp equipage was stacked in the Alumbagh. Three days' provisions were ordered to be carried in the havresacks, and every preparation for an advance into the city was made for the following day.

It will be well to pause here, to consider the circumstances under which Sir Colin Campbell undertook the relief of the Lucknow garrison.

On the morning of the 14th of November, the force was joined by several detachments of various regiments, some reserve Royal Artillery and Sappers, about 200 of the Military Train, most efficiently equipped and mounted as dragoons, and two Madras Horse Artillery guns.

The strength of the force was, at a rough calculation, as follows:

Naval Brigade and Artillery	.	400
Cavalry	.	900
Infantry	.	3,200
Sappers	.	200
Total . .	.	4,700 men.
Heavy guns . . .	.	12
Mortars	.	10
Light field guns . .	.	27
Total Ordnance pieces	.	49

Such was the available force, exclusive of the detachment left at Alumbagh.

With every precaution, and a force sufficient for the simple relief of the Lucknow garrison, Sir Colin's position was a most anxious one. Before moving from Cawnpore, it was a point of the greatest importance to settle whether he should first attack the Gwalior Contingent at Calpee, which daily threatened Cawnpore—for any delay in doing so might involve the fate of Lucknow, as reports were received that they were greatly pressed—or, leaving in Cawnpore as large a force as he could spare, proceed to Lucknow, and having relieved the garrison, return to Cawnpore: with the whole force at his disposal, it was impossible to hold Lucknow, as will be seen hereafter.

The Duke of Wellington wisely observed, "If the world was to be governed by principles, nothing would be more easy than to conduct even the greatest affairs; but in all circumstances, the duty of a wise man is to choose the lesser of any two difficulties which beset him."

Such was exactly Sir Colin Campbell's position. With nothing to guide him he chose what he considered the least evil; to leave a detachment at Cawnpore and proceed to the relief of Lucknow.

From the Alumbagh, communications, by means of the old-fashioned telegraph, had been opened with the Residency; and a programme of signals was adopted which would show to the beleaguered garrison not only our movements but our intentions.

Our advance on Lucknow was made from a different point from that taken by General Havelock; who threaded his way through the densest part of the city, and that most strongly defended by batteries and barricades: across the Charbagh Bridge.

At nine o'clock, the columns being formed, they struck across country direct for the Dil Khooshah House, which, with the Martiniere, both highly defensible buildings, were intended to form the basis of our operations during the attack on the numerous works on the canal and suburbs. These on the side of the Goomtee, though possessing a series of highly fortified posts, were more open, and could be carried in detail; while the river, though in some points fordable for cavalry, formed somewhat a protection to the right flank.

Arriving in the neighbourhood of the Dil Khooshah park, the advance was met by a sharp fire of musketry. Captain Remmington's Troop and No. 17 Battery were ordered to the front, supported by three regiments of infantry; a running fight was kept up to the park, into which the infantry, covered by the guns, advanced, driving the enemy from the house. We crossed the park at speed, to the enclosure round the Martiniere College; here the resistance was stouter, and a number of guns opened from the plain in front, covered from view by brushwood.

Captain Hardy, of the Royal Artillery, brought up a heavy howitzer, which, with the eleven field guns, kept up such a continued rattle, that the enemy quickly evacuated the college; the infantry, bounding over the wall, drove them from the enclosure at the point of the bayonet, while the cavalry pursued for a considerable distance.

Brigadier Hope's Brigade occupied the gardens and enclosures attached to the Martiniere, which were surrounded by a high stone wall, and abutted

upon the canal. Captain Remmington's Troop of
Horse Artillery was in the same position; Brigadier
Russell was on the left, in front of Dil Khooshah;
while Brigadier Little, with the cavalry and No. 17
Battery, occupied the plain in front of the Martiniere
—the position extending from the canal on the right
to the Dil Khooshah park wall on the left.

Sir Colin Campbell had sent orders that the
greatest care was to be taken to prevent the left
being turned; as this would not only have cut off
our communications with the Alumbagh, but also
our commissariat stores and reserve ammunition,
now only on the road. The latter, with the baggage
of the army, excepting the tents, were to be stowed
around the Dil Khooshah House; an elevated
position, strongly situated, and not liable to surprise. With a view to prevent any such cata-
strophe, Brigadier Russell pushed forward several
companies of infantry, and seized two villages on
the banks of the canal opposite the left; a move
of the utmost importance, considerably strengthening
our position.

These villages were held by the Sikhs, until the
force advanced into Lucknow.

In the mean time, the enemy were collecting in
large bodies in front of the centre, near the Bank

House; while it was impossible, from the mass of buildings, to see what mischief was brewing in the suburb. Captain Grant, of H. M.'s 9th Lancers, galloped gallantly to the front to reconnoitre, and was saluted with a perfect *feu de joie;* providentially without effect. Brigadier Little (9th Lancers) ordered an immediate advance of the centre, at speed; which, favoured by a rise in the ground, we were enabled to effect unseen, debouching on the level plain within seven hundred yards of the enemy, who were on the opposite bank of the canal.

A few rounds, well put, sent them scuttling back into the city. A second advance brought us to the canal bank; the bed of which, and some groves on the opposite side (from which a heavy fire was kept up on the villages held by Major Russell), were soon cleared. But as it was not intended at the time to hold so extended a position in that quarter as the whole length of the canal bank presented, which was within musketry range of the suburbs, Brigadier Little fell back to the Martiniere Compound, where orders were issued for a night bivouac.

Scarcely were the horses untraced, than a heavy attack was made on the position from the city. The force turned out like magic; Remmington was first upon the road and went well to the front, nearly up to the canal bridge, followed by the remainder of the artillery and cavalry. The infantry, as each successive column arrived on the plain, deployed along the banks of the canal, while the 53rd, 93rd, and 4th Sikhs, attacked with vigour the main body of the enemy and drove them back with slaughter, pursuing them beyond the canal.*

Brigadier Hope's Brigade, No. 17 Battery, and two of Captain Peel's Naval Brigade guns, with a troop of dragoons, bivouacked on the canal; but no further attack was made during the night.

The rear guard under Colonel Ewart, H. M.'s 93rd, with Captain Blunt's troop, and some guns of the Royal Artillery, had had no easy time of it. With the rest of the force they had got under arms on the morning of the 11th, during which day they were carrying on a continued series of skirmishes; not arriving at the Dil Khooshah until the night following.

---

* It was in this attack Captain Wheatley of the Carabineers, and Lieutenant Mayne, of the Bengal Artillery, acting Assistant Quartermaster-General, were killed; the former, by a shell which struck him; the latter, I believe, by a bullet while reconnoitring in front. Not many hours before, six of us, Wheatley and Mayne being of the number, were sitting under a hedge; a beautiful little bullock, chased by some soldiers, jumped into our circle; Wheatley caught him. It was unanimously voted that he should be kept for Christmas day, Wheatley adding, at the time, " I wonder how many of us will be alive." Both were gallant officers, and deeply regretted.

No further advance was made. On the 15th the commissariat and ordnance arrangements were completed at the Dil Khooshah, and H. M.'s 8th Foot, with the cavalry and three guns left for their custody; a road was cut from the Martiniere by the sappers, to the canal, near its junction with the Goomtee.* A desultory fire of musketry, varied by a shell or two from mortars, was kept up during the whole day.

The sailors on our right, with that universal talent they possess of turning their hands to anything, threw up a battery in front of their guns, and escaped with scarcely a casualty; while the artillerymen, less inclined to use the spade and pickaxe, had many men badly wounded. The conduct of the sailors was most amusing; a shot at a Pandy with a carbine, with but the slightest chance of success, was hailed with as great delight as a schoolboy's first shot at a crow; and to be without one for any length of time was a real hardship. Their fun and good-temper on all occasions made it quite delightful to serve near them; while to men who had

* Expecting an attack from the Cawnpore side, the enemy committed a fatal error, having dammed up the canal and broken all the bridges between Banks's House and the Charbagh Bridge, leaving the portion near the Goomtee perfectly dry. The banks not being steep, presented little difficulty to the passage even of heavy guns.

been many years in India, there was a freshness in their ways, which brought the dear old country more to our hearts than anything else possibly could have done.

They were described by the natives who first saw them, as "little men four feet high, and four feet in the beam; always laughing and dragging about their own guns." Although becoming slightly amphibious, the idiosyncrasies of their own profession were kept up to an an amusing extent. They paraded (I beg pardon, mustered) not in front of the camp, like the regiments, or, like the artillery, near their guns, but in the officers' lines astern; which they persisted was their quarter-deck. The boatswain piped all hands to grog.—But, as I feel I am getting out of my depth, I must leave the honest hearts of the *Shannon* to a more nautical pen than mine.

On the night of the 15th, the signals agreed upon with Sir James Outram and General Havelock, to announce our arrival and advance on the following morning, were made. An immense bonfire was burning on the top of the Martiniere, salvos of balloon shells were discharged, while Captain Peel's rocket cars poured their frightfully destructive contents into the devoted city.

Early on the following morning, the 16th October,

the heavy guns were withdrawn from the advanced picquets on the canal, as were the detachments which formed portions of Brigadier Hope's Brigade; while Brigadier Greathed, with the rest of the advanced force, remained in that position until mid-day, at which time we formed the rear guard of the column. The route of the attacking force lay towards the Goomtee; where, crossing the canal, a direct advance was made upon the Secunderbagh.

The position consisted of a high walled enclosure of strong masonry, 120 yards square, carefully loopholed all round, flanked at the corners by circular bastions, and containing inside a double story of houses, producing a double line of fire. In the centre was a two storied house, from which, and from the parapeted flat roof, a triple fire was kept up.

The entrance on the south side was carefully protected by a traverse of earth and masonry, to breach which would have been a work of time. On the north side was a small wicket, similarly protected; it was considered better to breach the main wall of the building. In front of the south side, at not 250 yards' distance, was a carefully loopholed serai,* while to the east and south the place was surrounded with villages supporting each other within musket range.

* Caravansery; resting-place for travellers.

The attack on this position Sir Colin Campbell thus describes:—

" On the head of the column advancing up the lane to the left of the Secunderbagh, the infantry of the advanced guard was quickly thrown in skirmishing order to line a bank to the right.

" The guns were pushed rapidly forward; namely, Captain Blunt's troop of Bengal Horse Artillery, Captain Travers's (Royal Artillery) Heavy Field Battery.

" The troops passed at a gallop through a cross fire from the village and Secunderbagh, and opened battery within easy musketry range in a most daring manner. As soon as they could be pushed up a stiff bank, two 18-pounders, under Captain Travers, were brought to bear upon the building.

" While this was being effected, the leading brigade of infantry, under Brigadier the Hon. Adrian Hope, coming rapidly into action, drove the enemy from the loopholed village.

" The whole fire of the brigade was directed on Secunderbagh.

" After a time, a large body of the enemy, who were holding ground to the left of our advance, were driven off by parties of the 53rd and 93rd; two of Captain Blunt's guns aiding the movement.

" A portion of the Highlanders pursued their advantage, and seized the barracks, immediately converting it into a military post; the 53rd, stretching in a long line of skirmishers in the open plain, driving the enemy before them.

" The attack on the Secunderbagh had now been proceeding for about an hour and a half, when it was determined to take the place by storm, through a small opening which had been made.

" This was done in the most brilliant manner by the remainder of the Highlanders, the 53rd and 4th Punjaub Infantry, supported by a battalion of detachments under Major Barnston.

" There never was a bolder feat of arms. The loss inflicted on the enemy, after the entrance of the Secunderbagh was effected, was immense. More than 2,000 of the enemy were carried out.*

" The officers who led these regiments were Lieutenant-Colonel L. M. Hay, H. M.'s 93rd Regt.; Lieutenant-Colonel Gordon, H. M.'s 93rd; Captain Walton, H. M.'s 53rd; Lieutenant Paul (since dead), 4th Punjaub Infantry; and Major Barnston, H. M.'s 90th Foot.

" Captain Peel's Royal Naval Siege Train then

---

* I was subsequently informed that upwards of 2,700 bodies were buried, and numbers more were burnt. The probability is that the enemy's loss was some 3,000 men.

went to the front towards the Shah Nujeef, together
with the Field Battery, and some mortars; the village
to the left having been cleared by Brigadier Hope
and Lieutenant-Colonel Gordon.

" The Shah Nujeef is a domed mosque with a garden, of which the most had been made by the enemy.
The walls of the enclosure were pierced by a double
tier of loop-holes. The entrance to it had been
covered by a regular traverse of earth and masonry;
the top of the building was crowned with a parapet.
From this, and from the defences in the garden, an
unceasing fire of musketry was kept up from the
commencement of the attack.

" This position was defended with great resolution
against a heavy cannonade of three hours. It was
then stormed by the 93rd Highlanders, under Brigadier Hope, and supported by Major Barnston's
battalion of detachments; Captain Peel led up his
guns with extraordinary gallantry within a few yards
of the building, to batter the massive stone walls.
The withering fire of the Highlanders effectually
covered the Naval Brigade from great loss. But it
was an action almost unexampled in war; Captain
Peel behaved himself very much as if he had been
laying the *Shannon* alongside an enemy's frigate.
This brought the day's operations to a close."

The rear-guard closed upon the Secunderbagh at about four in the afternoon. Seizing the opportunity of a moment's leisure, I ran inside to see a sight I was told would astound me, and even glut all revenge for the atrocious deeds of Cawnpore. It was indeed a massacre, such as no imagination could conceive. Within the enclosure, about 120 yards square, lay the dead bodies of about 3,000 sepoys, mostly bearing the mark of the deadly bayonet. Not a man, it is believed, escaped to tell the tale. Never was punishment so summarily inflicted. Its effect on the besieged was said to have been terrible. Four entire regiments were lost to them, at that post alone. When once the Highlanders got inside with the Sikhs, and the bayonet came into play, the enemy could not have had room to fight, while the crowd was increased by the terrified holders of the upper story rushing down below.

No. 17 Battery was immediately ordered up, to cover the withdrawal of the siege guns from the Shah Nujeef after the position had been stormed. This was only a precaution against any attack which might have been made upon them from the villages which extended far to our left front. None, however, was made. The appearance of the whole scene more resembled Dante's "Inferno" than anything earthly. The darkness of night had set in; but all was as light as day: the whole panorama was in a blaze. Shot and shell were flying about in all directions; the rattle of musketry never ceased; while the Highland yell and responsive British cheer, as the columns cleared the contested position, told that they had carried all before them.

In front, upon his horse, surrounded by the officers of his staff not wounded, sat Sir Colin Campbell; his knit brows telling how deep was his anxiety for the successful termination of the evening's work. No sooner did he hear the well-known yell of his pet Highlanders, his comrades in many a hard-contested field, then all trace of care vanished, and he calmly turned round to make his dispositions for the night, himself retiring to his bivouac near the Secunderbagh.*

The position of the force on the first night of the attack on Lucknow may be described as follows. Its right and most advanced post at the Shah Nujeef and Kadam Russool (Fort of the Prophet), which, although not before mentioned, was a mosque of considerable strength on an elevated position, which had been seized and occupied.

---

* Sir Colin loved a bivouac. When at the Martiniere, where a good house was over his head, he slept in the open air with all his staff; merely from sheer love of doing exactly as his troops did.

The centre was at the Secunderbagh, and on the plains in its front and left, while the extreme left was at the barracks; the position being somewhat of a semicircular shape: our communications during the whole time, by the untiring energies of the cavalry, were kept open with the Dil Khooshah park.

It was indeed a successful termination to the first attack: more was gained than could well be expected; but it was still clear that we should have to fight, as at Delhi, for every yard of the city. Sir Colin's principle of using shot instead of life was the salvation of hundreds, and the result was certain.

Musket bullets are not pleasant flying about, singing gaily as they pass; and a ten-inch shell plumping down among the hospital-litters and medical comforts makes one start a bit—eh, Doctor? But there is something undeniably horrible in the bang of a round shot; its very whiz at a distance makes you feel uncomfortable: nothing in reality is more destructive, and one thing only worse in sound; and that is one of Peel's rockets. Though on your own side, the very sight of the little car, with the mast slipt in its centre, makes your hair stand on end. Reader, if you ever see it coming near you (Peel in all probability will be whistling or telling some amusing anecdote—in fact, as much unconcerned as

[8]   L

if going to an evening party), and you are trying
to snooze off the effects of a hard day's work, quietly
move off as far as possible: your rest is gone. A
more diabolical apparatus for rousing an army from
its repose never was invented; but, abominable as is
the disturbance they make, their effect, as Peel used
them, must have been terrific in a crowded city.

From the position above described, it will be seen
that although our communications were open to our
rear, it was only through the one narrow lane
through which the attacking columns had advanced
on the Secunder Bagh.

The left, although occupying a portion of the
barracks, was still insecure, and liable to be turned
by troops at or near the hospital, or in the neighbourhood of the D Bungalows.*

On the morning of the 17th, Brigadier Russell,
with detachments of H. M.'s 82nd, 23rd, and 93rd
Highlanders, after considerable difficulty, occupied
these enclosures, and a detachment of the 2nd Punjaub Infantry was pushed forward to Banks' House,
thus securing our left flank and communications in
that direction with the rear.

---

* Four houses, formerly occupied by officers of H. M.'s 32nd,
marked D in original plan, have ever been known as the D
Bungalows.

While these operations were successfully carried on, on the left, the Naval Brigade and Mortar Batteries were at work bombarding the Mess House. This operation is thus described by Sir Colin Campbell:—

"This building, of considerable size, was defended by a ditch twelve feet broad and scarped with masonry, beyond that a loopholed mud wall. I determined to use my guns as much as possible in taking it.

"About 3 P.M. it was considered that a party might be sent to storm it without much risk; it was taken by a company of the 90th Foot under Captain Walmsley, and a picquet of H. M.'s 53rd under Captain Hopkins, supported by Major Barnston's battalion of detachments under Captain Guise, H. M.'s 90th Foot, and some Punjaub Infantry under Lieut. Powlett. The Mess House was carried with a rush.

" The troops then pressed forward with great vigour, and lined the wall separating the mess house from the Matee Mahal, which consists of a wide enclosure and many buildings. The enemy here made a last stand, which was overcome after an hour; openings having been broken in the wall, through which the troops poured, with a body of

L 2

Sappers, and accomplished our communications with the residency.

"I had the inexpressible satisfaction shortly afterwards of greeting Sir James Outram and Sir Henry Havelock, who came out to meet me before the action was at an end.

"The relief of the besieged garrison had been accomplished."

With what feelings of a soldier's pride and thankfulness of heart to the Disposer of all human affairs must these last lines have been penned. It was indeed a noble work, and done so successfully. Every point in the great game had been carried out as planned, and with perfect judgment. The enemy were completely checkmated.

Their victims, and the treasure for which their lustful hearts had sighed for months, would in a few hours glide safely from their grasp. Still, though communications were opened with the Residency, the most difficult operations had still to be carried out; namely the safe withdrawal of the garrison, with hundreds of women, children, sick, and wounded, ordnance, ammunition, Government records, treasure, and an immense quantity of commissariat stores.

These had all to be withdrawn in safety; first to

Cawnpore, and the sick, with the women and children, subsequently to Allahabad.

If coming to Lucknow, leaving the Gwalior Contingent in his rear, was the choice of two evils, Sir Colin Campbell had certainly now to exercise the deepest responsibility in the path before him. To use his own words, his army was continually one outlying picquet, without supports; nay, even without a main body: for seven days not a man had been off duty. Such a state of things could not continue, and to advance further into the city was only to increase the evil by spreading these picquets over a wider space.

On the other hand, to retreat before an Eastern enemy of overwhelming numbers—always a hazardous experiment—hampered as was the army with this immense train, would be peculiarly so.

In the face of the strongest opposition, Sir Colin determined to evacuate the city, and fall back on Cawnpore; the security of which station was essential to all future operations.

That his views and combinations were clear and masterly will be seen hereafter.

Although Brigadier Russell was in possession of the D Bungalows, he was exposed to such a fire of musketry from the surrounding buildings, extending from the point G to the mosque K, and along the

loopholed wall KH, as also to the fire of a battery
at the point M, containing an 18-pounder, that it
was impossible even to walk about beyond the protection of the thick mud walls of the enclosures.

Sir Colin Campbell's intention was not to be
dependent upon the single tortuous sandy lane, by
which he had advanced, for the withdrawal of the
besieged garrison; but, if possible, to command the
point M entirely, and take them out by the metalled
wide road NM, and thus to the Dil Khooshah bridge
over the canal, protected by the detachment sent previously into Banks' House.

The first object then was to silence the fire upon
Brigadier Russell's position. With this view, on
the morning of the 18th, I was directed to reconnoitre, in company with the late Colonel Biddulph,
the whole of the roads which formed a network
among the villages lying between the barracks
and the canal; with a view to discover whether
guns could not be taken down in safety to Colonel
Russell's assistance.

A road was soon found; a 9-pounder and a 24-
pounder howitzer, with four 5½-inch mortars, were
at once got into position in D 2 enclosure (as shown
in the plan), the mortars being placed behind the
house itself to shell the neighbourhood.

These operations were entirely carried on by hand: no mounted man could show without the certainty of a bullet. The iron 18-pounder was not above 120 yards distant, and to avoid giving notice to the enemy of our intentions by opening an embrasure, the muzzle of the 9-pounder was crammed through a hole that a shot had just made. The riflemen declared they had not been able to load again. As we fired so did they. A cloud of dust is all I remember: Brigadier Russell, Captain Ogilvie, and I were on our backs. Poor Russell had just been grazed on the back of the neck: the clods broken from the wall had knocked us over. Again and again we plied our gun with round shot, behind a charge of grape; they never again fired, and finally withdrew their gun.*

Lieutenant Burnett, of the Royal Artillery, in the meantime had got his mortars under weigh, and opened such a shower of shells upon our neighbours as soon greatly decreased the musketry fire, although not silencing it.

On Brigadier Russell being *hors de combat,* Colonel Biddulph, who hitherto had wandered about in a

---

* To have stormed the battery and taken the gun would have been uselessly sacrificing men's lives. It was commanded by hundreds of riflemen.

shower of bullets, as if they had no power over him, took command of the position, and organised a column to storm the hospital. As he was explaining his plans to Colonel Hale at the gate of D 3 enclosure, a bullet struck him dead; passing through his brain, but previously going through Hale's hat.*

Colonel Hale now took command. At 4 o'clock P.M., covered by a quick fire from the 24-pounder howitzer at the gate, and a flight of shells from the mortars, he led his column from D 3 enclosure into the gardens opposite, and so into the hospital; which was stormed and carried after a most stubborn resistance. Unfortunately the hospital was thatched, and being commanded by the loopholed parapet round the mosque K, and the buildings along the road leading to the Imambaras, it was soon in a tremendous blaze. From the heat alone it was impossible to remain there; Colonel Hale therefore formed up his men and withdrew them, in perfect order, to his original position, covered by the 24-pounder howitzer.†

---

* Hale seemed to have a charmed life: a round shot took his horse from between his legs; this bullet went through his hat, and a third just grazed his heels.

† Lieutenant Harrington, Bengal Art., and another officer (whose name I regret I never knew) belonging to H. M.'s Service, with a gunner of artillery and a drummer of infantry, did most gallant service. A man of the storming column had been wounded, and left in the garden for an hour and a half. The drummer

In the mean time an attack had been made upon the barracks on the right; encouraged no doubt by the retirement on the extreme left. It was quickly repulsed; the picquets having been strengthened, and Captain Remmington's troop sent to their support: which duty was carried out in a most dashing and gallant manner.

On the morning of the 18th the whole of the villages down to the canal bank were again carefully reconnoitred; and it was found that they contained a perfect network of roads: heavy, it is true, but sufficiently good for the transit even of heavy artillery. All thoughts, therefore, of withdrawing the garrison by the metalled road from the Secunder Bagh was abandoned, as it was evident that it would have entailed not only the retaking of the hospitals, but the Imambaras and the mosque O, which were again commanded by the Artillery from the Kaiser Bagh. Orders were therefore given to Colonel Hale simply to hold his present position; which, by the indefatigable industry of Captain Ogilvie, was entrenched so effectually, that it became a comparatively safe residence; although the musketry fire was never

stuck by him, and dashed into the picquet to report the fact. The little party above mentioned, under a very hot fire, rushed out, and brought in the wounded man. As they left the picquet a round shot struck the ground under their feet.

silenced.   Here we remained until the whole of the
troops had been withdrawn from the city.

One great advantage all must have felt was the
clearness with which all orders were issued by Sir
Colin, not only as to grand movements, but in every
detail.

On grand occasions, a confidential memorandum
having been prepared, commanding officers were
summoned, and each had the duty he had to per-
form explained to him.

General Mansfield's " Gentlemen, is there anything you do not understand?" was seldom responded
to.   Few ever took down "their parts" in writing.

Nothing can better describe the withdrawal of the
troops from Lucknow than Sir Colin Campbell's
despatch, as follows :—

" During the next three days, the 20th, 21st, and
22nd of November, I continued to hold the whole of
the country from the Dil Khooshah to the gates of
the Residency; the left flank having been secured in
the manner above mentioned, with the view to extri-
cating the garrison without exposing it to the chance
of even a stray musket-shot.

" From the first, all the arrangements have been
conducted towards this end.   The whole of the force
under my immediate command being one outlying

picquet, every man remained on duty, and was constantly subject to annoyance from the enemy's fire; but such was the vigilance and intelligence of the force, and so heartily did all ranks co-operate to support me, that I was enabled to conduct this affair to a happy issue, in exactly the manner originally proposed.

" Upon the 20th fire was opened on the Kaiser Bagh,* which gradually increased in importance until it assumed the character of regular breaching and bombardment.

" The Kaiser Bagh was breached in three places by Captain Peel, R.N., and I have been told that the enemy suffered much loss within its precincts. Having thus led the enemy to believe that an immediate assault was contemplated, orders were issued for the retreat of the garrison through the lines of our picquets at midnight on the 22nd.

" The ladies and families, the wounded, the treasure, and such guns as were thought fit to take away; the ordnance stores, the grain still possessed by the Commissariat of the garrison; and the state prisoners had all been previously removed.†

* Garden of the Cæsars.

† Although every precaution was taken, and every species of carriage available was placed at the disposal of the ladies, it was indeed a sad sight to see the shifts many were put to. I went

" Sir James Outram had received orders to burst the guns which it was thought undesirable to take away; and he was finally directed silently to evacuate the Residency of Lucknow at the hour indicated.

" The dispositions to cover their retreat and to resist the enemy should he attempt to pursue, were ably carried out by Brigadier the Hon. Adrian Hope; but I am happy to say the enemy was completely deceived, and he did not attempt to follow.

" On the contrary, he began firing on our old positions many hours after we had left them.* The movement of retreat was admirably executed, and was a perfect lesson in such combinations.

" Each exterior line came gradually retiring through its supports, until at length nothing remained but the last line of infantry and guns, with which I

once down to the Residency to see if I could assist any friend, and found Mrs. Fletcher Hayes, who had attempted to walk, seated on the steps of a house, with no means of getting on. Captain Ximenes, of H. M.'s 8th Regiment, an old friend, was with her. It was no time to hesitate ; so, although terribly exhausted, she mounted my horse. Lieutenant Hunter, of the Artillery, *shouldered* the baby; and off we all started. Before we brought her in safety to the Secunder Bagh many shot had flown past us, and nothing but the extreme danger of stopping on the road could have carried her through.

* Captain Waterman, 17th N. I., did not wake up when the rest of the garrison left the Residency, and in the morning found himself alone. His position was not an enviable one, but he escaped unhurt.

was myself to crush the enemy if he had dared to follow up the picquets. The only line of retreat lay through a long and tortuous lane, and all these precautions were necessary to ensure the safely of the force.

" The extreme posts on the left, under Lieutenant-Colonel Hale, H. M.'s 82nd, Lieutenant-Colonel Hales, H. M.'s 23rd Foot, and Lieutenant-Colonel Ewart, H. M.'s 93rd Highlanders, made their way by a road which had been explored for them; after I considered that the time had arrived, with due regard to the security of the whole, that their posts should be evacuated.

" It was my endeavour that nothing should be left to chance, and the conduct of the officers in exactly carrying out their instructions was beyond all praise. During all these operations, from the 16th instant, the remount of Brigadier Greathed's brigade closed in the rear, and now again formed the rear guard as we retired to Dil Khooshah; which was reached by the whole force by 4 A.M. on the 23rd instant."

Such were the operations by which, after a six months' imprisonment so touchingly described by General Inglis, the garrison of Lucknow were withdrawn. But the feelings of the liberated were not wholly pleasurable. How many had left within their late prison-house the last remains of those most dear to them. Many, many were the "Rachels weeping for their children" among that gallant band.

All had undergone the greatest hardships; wanting even the commonest necessaries of life. Beef and bread they had, it is true, and water; but none of the little comforts absolutely necessary in a warm climate, particularly for ladies and children.

Wonderful indeed was it that so many had escaped. The most exposed buildings were completely beaten to pieces with shot; the upper rooms of the residency were uninhabitable, and the lower rooms were riddled through and through. So short a distance were the besiegers from the besieged, that the former used to reproach the few sepoys who, through good and bad report, remained faithful to us, with being traitors to their cause, country, and religion.

Sir Henry Lawrence's dying moments were devoted to impressing his views and plans upon those who would succeed him in his capacity as Chief Commissioner and Commander; above all, knowing the treachery of the native mind, he besought them, as he had impressed on General Wheeler, never to dream of coming to terms; knowing full well what might be

expected as to the result. Proud indeed would he
have felt could he but have known that his wishes
were so nobly and manfully fulfilled.

The scene at the Dil Khooshah park was one of
the utmost confusion conceivable. Everything was
crowded into the smallest space; nothing was settled
for providing regularly for the wants of so many
hundred women and children. It was therefore
decided to start on the following morning for the
Alumbagh, abandoning the position at the Martiniere
and Dil Khooshah, and organising the arrangements
required on the large plain, where we had encamped
prior to entering Lucknow.

The march was accomplished without incident.
An officer was appointed to superintend the camp
arrangements for the released ladies and children.
Every mess was cheered by the presence of a certain
number, and each tried how much he could contri-
bute to their comfort and happiness.

But the brightness which surrounded the release
of the Lucknow garrison was dimmed by an event
which threw a gloom over the whole camp.

It was well known that General Havelock, worn
out by his exertions and the exposure he had suffered,
was much reduced by that terrible disease, so fatal
in the East, dysentery; but none imagined his end was

so near. Immediately on leaving the Residency he had been persuaded to go to the Dil Khooshah, hoping that the change and comparative quiet might arrest the disease.

On the morning of the 24th, that good man and soldier, not more devoted to his country than to his God, breathed his last; his work on earth just completed. He had seen the little band of his countrymen and country-women, for whom he had risked his life and his army, rescued from the fangs of a bloodthirsty enemy; who, too great cowards to rush upon their prey, only waited for the moment when famine would drive them to surrender. If anything on earth was necessary to comfort his departing spirit, the fulfilment of his most ardent hopes as to their relief must have soothed his last moments.

On the morning of the 26th November, his earthly remains, covered by the flag he had so nobly served, were deposited in a grave in the Alumbagh; followed by a large number of his brother officers, among whom were his son and Sir Colin Campbell. Though not actually dying on the field of battle, his was truly a soldier's death. No one who knew General Havelock as a Christian, could doubt, as his body was returning to the earth from whence it came, but that his would be a joyful resurrection, to inherit the promises made by his Heavenly Father from the foundation of the world.

The whole of the 25th and 26th were spent in reorganising the force and getting the camp equipage out of the Alumbagh.

In the meantime, it was determined to leave General Outram, who was also Chief Commissioner in Oude, with his brigade, at and around the Alumbagh, with a detachment some ten miles in his rear, in an entrenched position, holding the Bunnee bridge; thus showing that it was not intended entirely to abandon Oude. The presence of this force, amounting to about 3,000 men, with eighteen guns, would hold the city in check, and prevent any advance on Cawnpore from that direction.

On the morning of the 27th, leaving these detachments in his rear, Sir Colin Campbell, hampered as no army ever was before, with a train extending along, at least, ten miles of road, three deep, started for Cawnpore, to see what mischief was brewing in that direction.

CHAPTER XII.

DEFEAT OF THE GWALIOR CONTINGENT.

It will be remembered that the chief difficulty which, as a General, Sir Colin Campbell had to overcome in planning his advance on Lucknow was, how in the interim to dispose of the Gwalior Contingent; which on the banks of the Jumna at Kalpee, threatened the security of Cawnpore.

At the Alumbagh, that low tremulous sound, or rather vibration of the atmosphere, which, even at a distance of forty miles, to the practised ear denotes heavy firing, was plainly distinguishable.

No communication had been held with Cawnpore during the last week, but none doubted what was really the meaning of the sounds we heard; though few anticipated the disastrous scenes we were again about to enter upon.

The rear guard of Sir Colin's force, which left the Alumbagh at midday on the 27th, crawled along the road, following its immense amount of impediment, and did not arrive at the Bunnee bridge, where the camp was pitched, until midnight.

The firing, so faintly heard at the Alumbagh, was distinct at Bunnee. Orders were therefore issued for an advance on Cawnpore, a distance of thirty miles, on the following morning.

At sunrise, after threading our way with difficulty through the chaos of carts and baggage which encircled the camp like a mighty barricade, the columns were formed upon the road; they had not proceeded far, when the firing again commenced at Cawnpore, and continued nearly the whole of the day.

Up to 12 o'clock no intelligence was received as to what was actually going on; but, to quote Sir Colin's own words, shortly afterwards, " I received two or three notes in succession. 1st. That Cawnpore had been attacked. 2nd. That General Windham was hard pressed. 3rd. That he had been obliged to fall back upon his entrenchment."

Three salvoes were fired at about 2 P.M. from the battery, to intimate our approach; but it is doubtful whether they were ever heard, or if heard, understood.

It was not until the force arrived near the banks of the Ganges, on the evening of the 28th November, that the true state of affairs became known. Not only had General Windham retired upon his entrenchment, leaving the whole of his camp and baggage in the hands of the enemy, but the whole station and city, to within 200 yards of the field works, were also in possession of the enemy.

Sir Colin Campbell, with a few of his staff, crossed the bridge of boats at once. He was met by an officer, in a dreadful state of excitement, inquiring " Where Sir Colin was to be found. That they were at their last gasp," &c.

Things were certainly disastrous enough. Brigadier Carthew, that evening, withdrew from the church, theatre, and assembly rooms; all highly defensible posts: in the latter was stacked the whole of the baggage and camp equipage of General Havelock's force, left there when he crossed the Ganges into Oude; while in the enclosure around the assembly rooms, were pitched all the tents intended for the sick, wounded, and ladies of the relieved garrison.*

Once in the hands of the enemy their doom was sealed, and the flames, which during the night rose triumphantly to the skies, told of the havoc which was carrying on.

---

* The poor ladies were indeed to be pitied: only just withdrawn from one scene of desolation they were again plunged into a second of great danger.

The few buildings which, on the first recapture of
Cawnpore by General Havelock, had been saved,
were now destroyed, while a heavy fire was kept up
upon the entrenchments from ordnance of every
description, and musketry.

During the night, Sir Colin Campbell had made
all his arrangements for the morrow; but it is as well
to consider what would have been the state of the
country had he allowed his better judgment to have
been overruled, and remained, with the greater part
of his army, in Lucknow.

No idea can be formed of the disastrous consequences which would have ensued; in a short time
the bridge across the Ganges, if not in the hands of
the enemy, would have been under fire from any
amount of guns that they might choose to bring upon
it; perhaps totally destroyed. The army of Lucknow,
burdened with its frightful train, would have been
not only isolated from Cawnpore, but from the whole
of "India proper," and placed in the awkward predicament of being between two enemies, the Gwalior
Contingent and the rebel army in Lucknow; and in
a country, too, where every village was a fortified
enemy's position, and no supplies were procurable.

This was exactly the state of affairs Sir Colin
foresaw, and therefore hastened as much as possible

the withdrawal of the Lucknow garrison and his return to Cawnpore.

On the morning of the 29th November, he performed one of the most difficult of military operations, crossing a wide river in the face of an enemy thoroughly equipped with artillery. Providence, whose merciful hand has been so wonderfully extended over us during this critical year, alone prevented their having brought, during the 28th, their heavy artillery to command the bridge of boats and the road on the opposite bank approaching it.

Knowing that Sir Colin was on his return to Cawnpore, their not doing so was a mystery, only to be solved by the belief that, although for His inscrutable purposes the Almighty had allowed the scourge to pass over the land, yet He who had placed a bound to the ocean, had, in like manner, limited the successes of the enemy: the decree had gone forth, " So far shalt thou go and no further."

Early on the morning of the 29th, Captain Peel's heavy guns, with those attached to the Royal Artillery, were formed on the left bank of the Ganges, to cover the crossing of the troops, and prevent any attempt being made by the enemy to bring guns to the river side to command the bridge.

Brigadier Hope's Brigade, with Captain Remmington's Troop of Horse Artillery, No. 17 Battery, and some squadrons of dragoons, were the first to cross at 8 o'clock; being saluted as we passed the entrenchment by grape, fired high, fortunately, and doing little damage. The orders of the Commander-in-Chief were to take up an entirely defensive position on the plain near the dragoon barracks, extending towards the Allahabad road; thus preventing the possibility of any further advance of the enemy upon the eastern portion of the station and covering our communications towards Calcutta, whence our reinforcements were daily arriving. This movement was successfully carried out; the advance being also covered by the guns in the Fort. Picquets were pushed forward to within musket-range of the canal, occupying some ruined houses in our front.

The enemy in the mean time had brought some light guns into the suburbs of the city near the canal, which commanded the dragoon barracks; these formed good traverses for the protection of the troops, and little damage was done.

On the evening of the 29th, the artillery parks, the wounded and sick, and the families, commenced to cross the river; an operation which continued until 6 o'clock on the evening of the following day. The enemy during the 30th had attempted to bring guns to bear upon the bridge, as also to destroy it by fire-rafts, &c., but without effect.

On the 3rd December, the whole of the wounded, with the ladies, started for Allahabad. During the 5th and 6th, the field hospital was established in the Foot Artillery Barracks; and the Artillery park on the ground in the rear of the Foot Artillery Hospital.

During these six days we had been chafing and fretting at the proximity of the enemy, and the shot he kept continually bowling into the camp. Heavy gun batteries had been prepared to command the several canal bridges, and every precaution taken to secure the safety of our position. The picquets of the two armies were along the banks of the canal, extending from the new serai (K N) up to the Grand Trunk Road. Our main picquet being on the Trunk Road, near the racecourse, the next at Salvador House.*

At some points the rival picquets were not 120 near yards distant from each other.

On the night of the 5th, an attack was made upon our left picquets, which, after two hours cannonading, was repulsed.

---

* This was a large building which had been purchased by Government for the protection of hundreds of starving children who were daily brought in during the famine of 1836. These little vipers were now, in all probability, in arms against us.

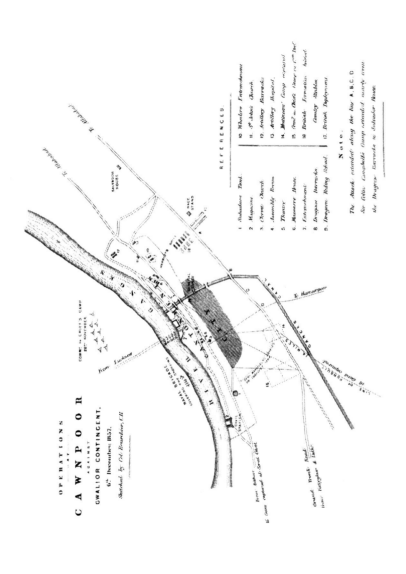

OPERATIONS
AT
CAWNPOOR
AGAINST
GWALIOR CONTINGENT.
6th December, 1857.

Sketched by Col. Beaucher, CB

REFERENCES.

1 Subadar's Tank.
2 Magazine.
3 Christ Church.
4 Assembly Room.
5 Theatre.
6 Massacre House.
7 Entrenchment.
8 Dragoon Barracks.
9 Dragoon Riding School.
10 Wheeler's Entrenchment.
11 St. John's Church.
12 Artillery Barracks.
13 Artillery Hospital.
14 Mutineers' Camp captured.
15 Posn. on Chalk Camp on 6th Dec.
16 Brigade Formation halted.
17 British Deployment.
   Cavalry Stables.

Note.

The Attack extended along the line A. B. C. D.
Sir Colin Campbell's Corps extended nearly over
the Dragoon Barracks to Subadar Tank.

The Commander-in-Chief was now in a very different position from that in which he found himself on arriving at Cawnpore. Disagreeable as was the delay, to use his own words, it was precisely one of those cases in which no risk must be run. So far he had played his game on the defensive, now, it was his innings; and the lion which for six days had been fretfully pacing his narrow den, gathered up for a vigorous attack.

On the morning of the 6th, Sir Colin explained his views to commanding officers, as usual, from a memorandum before prepared, with a clearness none could mistake. The camp was struck at sunrise and sent to the rear, and all prepared for what my worthy friend "the doctor" *par excellence* used to term "a rubbing hands day."* The despatches tell the best tale of the fight :—

"The enemy's left occupied the old cantonment from which General Windham's post had been principally assailed; his centre was in the city of Cawnpore, and lined the houses overhanging the canal.

"His right stretched some way beyond the angle

---

* Explanation seems necessary. The above quaint term arose from numbers of our friends rubbing their hands with delight at the first sound of a brush.

formed by the Grand Trunk Road and the canal, two miles in rear of which the camp of the Gwalior Contingent was pitched, and so covered the Calpee road, the line of retreat of that body. In short, the canal, along which were placed his centre and right, was the main feature of his position, and could only be passed in the latter direction by two bridges.

"It appeared to me, that if his right was vigorously attacked, it would be driven from its position without assistance coming from other parts of the line. The walls of the town, which gave cover to attacking columns on our right, being an effective obstacle to the movement of any part of his troops from his left to right.

"Thus the possibility became apparent of attacking his division in detail.

"From intelligence received before and after the action, there seems to be little doubt that, in consequence of the arrival of four regiments from Oude, and the gathering of various mutinous regiments which had suffered in previous actions, as well as the assemblage of all the Nana's followers, the strength of the enemy now amounted to 25,000 men; with all the guns belonging to the Gwalior Contingent, some thirty-six in number, together with a few guns belonging to the Nana.

" Orders were given to General Windham on the morning of the 6th, to open a heavy bombardment at 9 A. M. from the entrenchment in the old cantonment, and so induce the belief that the attack was coming from the General's position.

" Brigadier Greathed, reinforced by the 64th Regiment,* was directed to hold the same ground opposite the centre of the enemy, which he had been occupying for some days past; and at 11 A. M. the rest of the forces as below,† was drawn up in contiguous columns in rear of our old cavalry lines, and effectually masked from the observation of the enemy. The cannonade from the entrenchments having become slack at this time, the moment had arrived for the attack to commence.

* *Brigadier Greathed's Brigade.*—H. M.'s 8th Foot, 64th Foot, 2nd Punjaub Infantry.

† *Artillery Brigade.*—2 Troops Horse Artillery, 3 light field batteries, guns of Naval Brigade, heavy field battery, Royal Artillery.

Cavalry Brigade.—H. M.'s 9th Lancers, detachments 1st, 2nd, and 5th Punjaub Cavalry and Hodson's Horse.

4th Infantry Brigade.—H. M.'s 53rd Regiment, H. M.'s 42nd and 93rd Highlanders, 4th Punjaub Rifles.

5th Infantry Brigade.—H. M.'s 23rd Fusiliers, H. M.'s 32nd Regiment, H. M.'s 82nd Regiment.

6th Infantry Brigade.—2nd and 3rd battalions Rifle Brigade, detachment H. M.'s 38th Foot.

Engineer Brigade.—Royal Engineers and Detachments Bengal and Punjaub Engineers, Sappers and Miners attached to the various brigades of infantry.

"The cavalry and horse artillery were sent to make a detour on the left and cross the canal by a bridge a mile and a half up, and threaten the enemy's rear.

"The infantry deployed in parallel lines facing the canal.

"Brigadier Hope's Brigade was in advance in our line, Brigadier Inglis' Brigade being in rear of Brigadier Hope. At the same time Brigadier Walpole, assisted by Captain Smith's Field Battery, Royal Artillery, was directed to pass the bridge immediately on the left of Brigadier Greathed's position, and to drive the enemy from the brick-kilns, keeping the walls of the city for his guide.

"The whole attack then proceeded; the enemy quickly responded from his proper right to the fire of our heavy and light artillery.

"The Sikhs of the 4th Punjaub Infantry, thrown into skirmishing order, supported by H. M.'s 53rd, attacked the enemy in some old mounds and brick-kilns to our left with great vigour.

"The advance then continued with rapidity along the whole line, and I had the satisfaction of observing, in the distance, Brigadier Walpole was making equal progress in the right.

"The canal bridge was quickly passed, Captain

Peel leading over it with a heavy gun, accompanied by a soldier of H. M.'s 53rd, named Hannaford.

" The troops which had gathered together resuming their line of formation with great rapidity on either side as soon as it was crossed, and continuing to drive the enemy at all points; his camp being reached and taken at 1 o'clock P.M., and his rout complete along the Grand Trunk Road.

" I must here draw attention to the manner in which the heavy 24-pounders were impelled and managed by Captain Peel and his gallant sailors.

" Through the extraordinary energy and good-will with which the latter have worked, their guns have been constantly in advance throughout our late operations, from the relief of Lucknow till now, as if they were light field-pieces, and the service rendered by them in clearing our front has been incalculable.

" On this occasion there was the sight beheld of 24-pounder guns advancing with the first line of skirmishers.

" Without losing any time, the pursuit was pressed with the greatest eagerness to the 14th milestone on the Calpee road; and I have reason to believe that every gun and cart of ammunition which had been in that part of the enemy's position which had been attacked, now fell into our possession."

On passing the camp of the enemy, Sir Colin Campbell directed General Mansfield to attack the enemy's position on the left, at the Subadar's Tank. This was also carried, after a stout resistance; but the main body of the enemy's artillery in that position had made off towards Bithoor.

Such was the defeat of the Gwalior Contingent; 16 guns, 350 cartloads of ammunition, the whole of their immense stores of grain, tents, bullocks, in fact everything they possessed, fell into our hands. Taken by surprise as to the point of attack, the rout and pursuit was the most complete thing imaginable; except in one respect. The cavalry, who had been directed with the Horse Artillery to threaten the right flank of the enemy, were taken by the guides a wrong road, and did not come up until the pursuit had been carried on some distance on the Calpee road.

Had they been present when the camp was stormed, an immense number of the enemy, who scattered all over the plain, might have been cut up. As it was, the pursuit was indeed a glorious termination to our day's work.

I can give no better idea of the orders I received than in the words of the adjutant of the Horse Artillery, Lieutenant Bunny; whose unbounded spirits under the most depressing circumstances were so enviable.

After about half an hour's heavy firing and crossing the canal, I met him coming back for me at full gallop. All he said was, "Come along, they are bolting like the devil." Away we went along the Trunk Road at a gallop; Peter Sconse, as was his wont when shot were flying about, yelling with delight. The infantry made way for us, and a mile and a half ahead we came upon the enemy's camp, and at 400 yards poured round shot into the flying masses before us. "Go to grape distance," was Major Turner's order; we limbered up, and from a distance of not more than 200 yards poured a shower of grape into their position. The men were yelling with delight; they actually stood upon the gun-carriages as we advanced; the drivers cheered, and such a scene of excitement was never known.

At the enemy's camp, Sir Colin himself came into the battery and gave orders for the pursuit. Hurrah! hurrah! we are on their track: gun after gun is passed and spiked, cartloads of ammunition lay strewed along the road; Pandies are bolting in all directions. For two miles without a check, the pursuit was carried on by the battery alone, accompanied by Sir Hope Grant and his Staff. Four

times in that distance did we come into action, to
clear our front and flanks; until General Grant,
thinking wisely that we were too far from our supports, determined to wait until the cavalry arrived.
A halt was called; not until it was required, for the
horses, though in the condition of racers, had felt
the pace. A small cloud coming nearer and nearer
is seen on the left. The head of the cavalry column
debouches from a grove. The order for a further
pursuit is given. The cavalry spread like lightning
over the plain, in skirmishing order. Sir Colin takes
the lead. The pursuit is continued to the 14th milestone; assuming all the character of a fox-hunt.
Strange to say, not many miles beyond the enemy's
camp, a fox broke right in front of the column; and a
view halloa told Reynard that the heavy crops would
be his safest refuge.

At the 14th milestone, on the banks of the Pandoo
River, the pursuit ceased, not a trace either of an
enemy, or a cart of any kind being in sight. The
column returned to the enemy's position on the junction of the Calpee and Cawnpore roads, to bivouac
for the night; arrangements being made for collecting the spoils of the enemy.

When it is known that on this day only one
week's supplies were in our camp, and that while the

Gwalior Contingent held the city and surrounding country, no more were procurable, it will be seen how important was the result of our victory. Thousands of fine bullocks fell into our hands. A reward of three rupees a head was offered those who might bring them in; the consequence was a series of the most absurd scenes. At the tail of each gun and waggon were tied three or four pairs of bullocks, while on each side of the road might be seen parties of Lancers driving hundreds before them; and here and there a sturdy gunner, mounted in triumph on a rampant bull, which was led by a couple of his comrades.

On the morning of the 7th of December, a column was formed, under General Hope Grant, to follow up the portion of the enemy who had escaped towards Bithoor and Futtehghur.

After a forced march of twenty-five miles, the column came upon the enemy as they were endeavouring to cross their guns at Serai Ghat, over the Ganges. General Grant's force consisted of Captain Middleton's Field Battery, Captain Remmington's Troop Horse Artillery, the 4th Brigade of Infantry, 2,054 strong, and 551 Cavalry; 100 sappers also accompanied the force. After reconnoitring the enemy, General Grant brought up his artillery,

[8]   N

which soon silenced the enemy's guns; the whole of which, fifteen in number, with an equal number of ammunition waggons, fell into his hands, and a considerable quantity of ammunition. The whole of the captured guns, &c., were sent into Cawnpore. General Grant returned at the same time, leaving Brigadier Hope in command of the column; which fell back on Bithoor, the residence of the accursed Nana. Here an immense deal of treasure, the property of his adopted father, was found in a well.

Thus ended all military operations for the present. On the morning of the 12th, the camp was shifted to Nawabgunge, the old Civil Station. On the 18th, a force consisting of troops as below* started under Brigadier Walpole, to restore confidence and British rule among the provinces bordering on the left banks of the Jumna.

* No. 17 Battery, Captain Blunt's Troop Horse Artillery, two battalions of Rifle Brigade, one regiment of H. M.'s Infantry, one company Sappers.

CONCLUDING CHAPTER.

THE column thus formed left Cawnpore at about 10 A.M. of the 18th December, on quite a holiday excursion. With the exception of a few sepoys, who were caught and hung in the villages, the whole population flocked to meet us.

For years, in fact, never had they seen so large a force of European troops. Though often molested by the cavalry of the Nana, they did not seem to have suffered any great amount of damage to their towns and villages. At the second march at Akbarpore we were informed that they had been well able to defend themselves and their property.

Sporting in all its branches took the place of fighting: it was really a blessing to be beyond the reach of round shot and musketry, and to enjoy heaven's fresh air in peace and quietness. In the morning we marched off with our bands all playing, and in the evenings lounged about the camp, listening to the last new opera airs just out from home.

N 2

Nothing particular occurred until the 29th December, when the column marched into the Civil Station of Etawah, which had been plundered early in the mutiny, like all other small stations unprotected by European troops. It was a wreck: the church, court-houses, and private residences, were in ruins.

A force of the enemy had only left the night before; but a few desperadoes were still hemmed into a walled enclosure: they had, indeed, selected a stronghold under one of the bastions which flanked each corner. For three hours they kept the whole brigade at bay, wounding several men with their muskets. Their position might have been stormed, but only with the loss of several men. We tried every expedient to dislodge them—hand-grenades, burning straw, &c.—but with no avail; at last nothing was left but to blow in the whole bastion. For this purpose, with Scatchley, of the Engineers, I made a mine in the roof, from a number of my gun cartridges; its explosion was most successful: it buried our friends below. About twenty were taken out of the ruins, with unfortunately two or three women and children. A number of men implicated in the mutiny were caught and hung. Every confidence was shown on the part of the Nawab (who from the first had been well affected) as to his being able to hold his own against any straggling bodies of the enemy, now that their main force and guns had been driven from the station.   Our letters, which for weeks had not been received, had been here concealed by the former native postmaster, and brought into camp hidden under the packsaddles of some donkeys.

Not the least dangerous trade during the mutiny was carrying letters for the British Government or private individuals.   Fabulous prices were paid for the transmission of a note.   All sorts of schemes were devised; but many poor fellows paid the penalty.   One man who fell into the hands of the Nana had his hands and nose cut off, and was sent back to our camp.

At Etawah we were within the clutches of the Agra Government, who apparently were in as anxious a state as when we left them on the 14th of October.*

Peremptory orders were received by Brigadier Walpole from the Chief Commissioner to leave the greater portion of his force at Etawah.   Fortunately

---

* A Cossid came into camp with a note from ——, a high functionary at Agra, saying, "that they were without information; that they had heard of dire disasters at Cawnpore, and if the British rule was gone, &c.: in fact, any information was better than nothing."   The Cossid, with his tongue in his cheek, added, "But mind, the Sahib told me if affairs were not so bad not to show the note, as they would be so laughed at."   He guessed wisely: they were well laughed at.

he was acting under direct orders from the Commander-in-Chief, which were paramount.

On the 20th January we marched into Mynpoory, which Brigadier Seaton's column had only left a few days previous. Here orders awaited us to join the Head-Quarters Camp without delay, which was *en route* to Futtehghur. On the 3rd January Sir Colin Campbell defeated the enemy with great slaughter, capturing twelve guns: they had attempted to arrest his advance into Futtehghur. The Nawab of Futtehghur, after blowing up his own palace (why, it is not known), escaped across the Ganges into Oude. By the side of the house was a gallows: the use it had been put to was but too well known.

On the 3rd we marched from Mynpoory to Bewar, where we found Brigadier Seaton's column encamped.

On the following morning both columns marched to Futtehghur, where Sir Colin Campbell had arrived the previous day.

It was reported that the chief instigator of all the cruelties of Futtehghur, Nazir Ali Khan, was still in the city; which was threatened with immediate bombardment, should he not be delivered up. On the morning of the 4th he was brought into camp. A more horrible specimen of a licentious Mussulman never was seen. He was surrounded, and with difficulty saved from the clutches of the sailors, who would have robbed the gallows of their due.

Strange was the infatuation of the Futtehghur mutineers: they must have fancied that the British power was finally crushed. The invaluable stock of timber belonging to the Gun Carriage Agency was untouched, as were the stores of clothing for the army.

Guns were mounted at the Agency House to command the passage of the river; yet the fort itself was not defended for a moment, but was evacuated even before Sir Colin had marched into the station.

The houses and church were here also utterly a wreck, the racket-court alone was standing. The tombstones in the burial-ground had not been spared, and all bespoke the havoc which had been committed upon all that bore the mark of an Englishman upon it.

Two dear friends, with their families, had here met their end. Major Robertson, wounded, had escaped across the river; but he subsequently died at the residence of a rich native who held his own in Oude, siding with the British Government. His wife and baby were drowned by his side, as was also his cousin. The Rev. Frederick Fisher was,

with his wife, also drowned in the river. These
ladies had all trusted to the stream sooner than to
the mercies of the sepoys.

My narrative has now come to a close. Sir Colin
Campbell having determined to collect his troops
at Cawnpore, to return to Lucknow for the complete subjugation of Oude, directed all officers not
directly belonging to troops in the field to join
their appointments, as a long delay must occur
ere hostilities would be recommenced.

It was with conflicting feelings that on the 13th
January I most unexpectedly received orders to
join a troop of Horse Artillery at Lahore. It
would be folly to deny that the thought of again
seeing those dear ones from whom I had been so
many months separated were not most delightful;
but it was not without deep pain that I parted
with my comrades, with whom eight such eventful
months had been spent, and to whose consideration
and kindness I was so deeply indebted. But among
all the good friends I left, old No. 17 claimed a first
place in my heart; and whatever may be my lot, I
can never forget the gallantry of those good officers
and soldiers who, under every circumstance, whether
of hardship or victory, conducted themselves in a
manner that to my dying day will make me feel

proud of my command during the eventful year of 1857.

On the following morning, the 14th, a convoy left Futtehghur for Allyghur, and to its tender mercies I entrusted my horses and other property; but as I was to go, the quicker I got over the ground the better. I mounted the mail cart at Bewar after a thirty mile ride, and on the 18th found myself at Simla, surrounded by the now happy faces of my wife and chicks.

One word more. If I felt gratitude towards my friends, and those with whom I had been so long associated, can I forget to return thanks to the Almighty, who, through such dangers, had surrounded us with mercies, and who had not suffered us to fall into the hands of the enemy.

———

Since the above was written I have been favoured with the following detailed account of the mutiny at Cawnpore, written by one who had access to the best sources of information. It will form an appropriate conclusion to this volume.

THE MUTINY AT CAWNPORE.

It is proposed in the following narrative to give a complete but succinct account of the occurrences connected with the mutiny of the native regiments at Cawnpore, and the disastrous consequences that ensued to the European inhabitants of the station.

It will not be an object to account in any way for the origin of the mutiny, or to investigate the causes that prompted native troops, on whom every reliance had been placed, to raise so formidable a rebellion.

Neither will it, perhaps, be desirable to enter into a detailed account of cases of individual suffering, a record of which may be placed more appropriately in an appendix to the narrative; where also may be found the records of survivors and others from which the information now furnished is gathered.

It is necessary, however, to describe the position of the rebel, who, if he did not from the first foster the mutiny, soon placed himself at the head, and by his intelligence and importance gave a plan and system to the revolt.

Nana Dhoondoo Punt was the adopted son of Bajee Rao, ex-Peshwa of Poonah, a pensioner of the British Government, who died in December, 1852.

The pension of the ex-Peshwa, amounting to eight lakhs of rupees per annum, was not continued to the Nana, and this appears to have been his principal, if not sole grievance; though he invariably maintained friendly relations with the European residents, and, indeed, on many occasions treated them with apparent cordial hospitality.

His residence was at Bithoor, situated ten miles west of Cawnpore, where he owned an estate left him by his patron, the ex-Peshwa. He was allowed a retinue of 500 infantry and cavalry, with three guns of small calibre; these troops being, of course, entirely independent of European authority.

Cawnpore, the head-quarters of a division of the army, is a large station some five miles in length, situated on the right bank of the Ganges; and though it was formerly occupied by a strong force of Europeans, the number of these had lately been reduced.

At the time of the revolt, the European force, including the reinforcements they received, consisted of

> Artillery, 1 co., 59 men and 6 guns.
> Infantry, 60 men of H. M.'s 84th.
> Infantry, 30 men of H. H.'s 32nd, invalids and sick.
> Infantry, 15 men of 1st Madras Fusiliers.

The native troops consisted of two regiments of Light Cavalry, the 1st, 53rd, and 56th Regiments of Infantry, and the Golundauze or native gunners attached to the battery.

General Sir Hugh Wheeler commanded the division, and a list of his staff and other officers will be found elsewhere.

There was a large number of Europeans resident in cantonments; many of whom were individuals connected with the civil, railway, canal, and other departments; there were also nearly the whole of the soldiers' wives of H. M.'s 32nd Regiment, which was stationed at Lucknow. The whole number of the European population, therefore, in Cawnpore, men, women, and children, could not have amounted to less than 750 souls.

News of the outbreak at Meerut and Delhi reached Cawnpore on the 14th of May; and though the mistrust prevailing more or less throughout the Bengal

Presidency was felt at Cawnpore—more especially with reference to the cavalry and the 1st Regiment N. I., who had been cantoned together for one year, and whose seditious feelings had been pretty openly expressed—no precautionary measures were adopted, except that the Artillery was moved up to the European barracks: and this movement was caused by a supposed incendiary fire, which occurred in the lines of the 1st Regiment N. I., on the night of the 16th of May.

The ladies and merchants also about this time sought refuge in the barracks. A company of H. M.'s 32nd Regiment arrived from Lucknow, and officers of all corps were ordered to sleep in the lines of their regiments. Further cause of alarm was given by rumours having been circulated in the city that objectionable cartridges were to be served out on the 23rd of May, and that the Artillery were to act against all who refused them. A good deal of excitement prevailed, and on the 24th of May, the Queen's birthday, it was not considered advisable to fire the usual salute.

The Nana had offered to protect the treasury in case of an outbreak; and on the 26th of May, at the request of the collector, he brought two guns and 200 Nujeebs (armed retainers), and placed them on guard on the Treasury, which was also guarded by a company of the 53rd N. I.

The 2nd Regiment Oude Cavalry, under the command of Lieutenant Barber, 30th N. I., marched into cantonments, and furnished patrols, together with a picquet of the 2nd Cavalry.

A few days after their arrival, the Oude Irregulars were inspected, and were accordingly marched out towards Futtehghur. Captain Hayes, 62nd N. I., Military Secretary to Sir H. Lawrence, Commander of Oude, and Captain Cary, 17th N. I., accompanying them; and they were followed, a day or two later, by Lieutenant Ashe, with a half battery of the Oude Horse Artillery.

A few marched from the station; but the cavalry regiment mutinied, and succeeded in murdering all the officers who were with them. Some Sikhs in the regiment, however, returned towards Cawnpore, and met and brought back Lieutenant Ashe and the guns. General Wheeler dismissed the Sikhs, and commenced intrenching the barracks of the depôt of H. M.'s 32nd; to which all the Europeans at the station were ordered to repair.

On the 2nd of June the first reinforcements arrived, consisting of two companies of H. M.'s 84th and fifteen men of the Madras Fusiliers. One company of the

former, with the company of H. M.'s 32nd, which had
arrived a few days before, were sent on to Lucknow.

On the 4th of June provisions for a month had
been stored, and one lakh of rupees was removed
within the intrenchments; but nine lakhs still remained
in the Treasury. No steps were taken to remove or
secure the ammunition and stores; which were lying
in large quantities both in the ordnance and regi-
mental magazines. It is necessary to mention this
fact to show, not only that full confidence was placed
in the Nana, but that no very serious view was taken
of matters in general. The officers of the 2nd company, and 1st and 56th Regiments N. I., were ordered
to discontinue sleeping in their lines.

The mutiny commenced on the morning of the 6th,
at 2 A.M., when the 2nd Cavalry and 1st Regiment
N. I. left their lines; without, however, molesting
their officers, who on the first alarm had proceeded
to their lines. The insurgents proceeded first to the
Treasury and Magazine, which were situated in the
civil lines of the western end of the station; they
obtained possession of both of these buildings without
any opposition from the guards placed over them.
They then entered the gaol, set the prisoners at
liberty, and burnt all the adjacent public offices and
records. They afterwards marched out to Kullum-

pore, the first halting place on the road to Delhi, and there encamped; being joined, before noon of the same day, by the 53rd and 56th Regiments Native Infantry.

Seizing the opportunity of the revolt, the Nana possessed himself of a great portion of the Treasury; then repairing to the rebel camp, he persuaded them to return to Cawnpore, to destroy the houses situated therein, and annihilate the British officers and soldiers, and every Christian resident, and then proceed to Delhi or Lucknow; leaving a garrison behind to retain possession of the city and district of Cawnpore.

Acting on his advice, and placing themselves under his orders, the rebels returned to Cawnpore the same evening. The Nana at once informed General Wheeler that he had returned to attack him.

Intimidating all natives of any standing or importance, plundering everything in his way, and murdering every European who fell into his hands, the Nana soon made good his word, by bringing into position two of his own guns, and two heavy guns which he had procured from the Magazine.

The cannonade from these guns commenced about 10 A.M., on the morning of the 7th June.

It is necessary, in order to render evident the situation of the besieged, to give a short account of the unfortunate position that had been selected by General Wheeler, and of the inadequate means that had been taken to secure it.

The depôt of H. M.'s 32nd Regiment, consisting of the sick, invalid women and children of the regiment, was located in two long barracks, in an extensive plain at the eastern end of the station. These barracks were single-storied buildings, intended each for the accommodation of a company of 100 men; one of them was thatched, and both were surrounded by a flat-roofed arcade, or verandah; the walls were of brick, one and a half thick; a well, and the usual out-offices were attached to the buildings.

Around these barracks a trench was dug, and the earth thrown up on the outside, so as to form a parapet; which might have been five feet high, but was not even bullet-proof at the crest; open spaces were likewise left for the guns, which were thus entirely unprotected. It may be imagined what slight cover an entrenchment of this kind would furnish, either for the barracks or for men in the trenches; while there was plenty of cover, both for musketry and guns, within a short distance of the barracks, of which the mutineers soon availed themselves.

[8]   o

To enclose the barracks, a parapet was required, and it is supposed that scarcity of labour, and the stiffness of the soil, which at the close of the hot season were nearly as hard as rock, were the causes which prevented the construction of more solid defences.

The cannonade commenced from the four guns before mentioned; but the enemy's artillery was soon strengthened from the Ordnance Magazine, and in a few hours they brought a fire on the barracks, on all sides, from fourteen guns and mortars in position.

At first the besieged replied briskly to the fire of the rebels, but without any signal success; for the guns in the entrenchments were field guns, and the enemy had not as yet advanced within 1,000 yards from the barracks. The fire of the rebels also had little or no effect; but on the second day of the siege they adopted more energetic measures: the Mahomedan flag was raised in the city; all true Mussulmans were directed to join, and those who demurred were threatened, insulted, or fined. The Nana's force was soon augmented by large numbers, and reinforced daily.

Having at his command a magazine stored with every description of ammunition and ordnance, with his treasury full, and the city bazaar in his hands, it is not to be wondered at that he soon rendered the situation of the Europeans next to hopeless. An incessant fire of musketry was poured into the entrenchments from the nearest buildings; guns of large calibre, drawing gradually closer and closer, sent their shot and shell, without intermission, against the brick walls of the barracks; and carcases fired the thatched buildings, in which numbers of sick and helpless women and wounded men were huddled together, many of whom were burnt alive!

The hospital stores were lost or destroyed, and all being now crowded into one building, without medicine, the sick and wounded died without relief. With the greater portion of their ammunition spent, the besieged were also forced to slacken their fire. In short their position was rendered hopeless and helpless in the extreme; and all this before the firing had lasted for half a week.

There was a nullah or ditch some distance in front of the intrenchments, by which the enemy pushed on a sap towards the barracks; and from this they poured in a near and deadly fire.

On the west of the besieged an entirely new range of barracks had been in the course of construction, and behind the unfinished walls the rebels posted their matchlockmen. They were, however, dislodged by sortie after sortie; and at length two of the barracks were held by picquets from the garrison. But the strength of the garrison was insufficient to prevent the rebels from placing their matchlockmen on the other side. Communications between the barracks became difficult; no one could move out of cover for one instant without drawing on himself the fire of twenty pieces. Water was at first drawn under shelter of the parapet at the edge of the well; but the parapet was knocked over, and soon not a drop could be obtained, save at the risk of almost certain destruction.

The half-destroyed walls of the barracks, or the temporary expedient of piling up tents and casks, formed the precarious but only shelter that could be obtained. Food could only be carried from post to post by day; and the dead were removed at night, and thrown into an adjacent well without the decency of burial.

Relief was expected on the 14th June; but day after day brought no succour. Round shot and disease were doing their work; provisions ran short; and the misery endured by all can hardly be imagined.

Yet the besieged, in successful sallies, took and spiked the nearest guns; driving away the mutineers and retiring, with little if any loss, to the trenches.

But the guns were either repaired, or replaced by others from the arsenal. Still, though the position in the barracks was quite untenable, the mutineers never mustered the courage to assault it.

Nor were the Europeans in the trenches the only sufferers. Besides several Europeans captured in the city, many of the natives suspected of aiding or serving the British Force were put to death. A list was made of all the bankers, who were mulcted of their wealth, and property of every description was. plundered or wantonly destroyed by the rebels.

Up to the 26th June, however, the British force held their own; though their loss in killed alone was upwards of 100, and the ladies and others were maddened by suffering.

It can scarcely be wondered at, that when, on that morning, the Nana offered to treat, his proposition was listened to. It was worded as follows:—

"All soldiers and others unconnected with the works of Lord Dalhousie, who will lay down their arms and give themselves up, shall be spared and sent to Allahabad."

Captain Moore, commanding the detachment of H. M.'s 32nd, who had from the first directed the energies of the besieged, and invariably led their sallies, seeing the reduced state of the beseiged, and relying on the word of the Nana, obtained permission to sign the paper; and, contrary to the advice and remonstrances of many other officers, the treaty was agreed to.

Boats were immediately provided for the conveyance of the remains of the garrison to Allahabad, and to these boats they proceeded on the morning of the 27th of June.

And now followed the most dastardly piece of treachery that has perhaps ever been perpetrated. Hardly had the party taken their places in the boats, when, by previous arrangement, the boatmen set the thatched awnings of the boats on fire, and rushed on to the bank. A heavy fire of grape and musketry was then opened on the Europeans. Out of thirty boats two only managed to start; one of these was shortly swamped by round shot, but its passengers were enabled to reach the leading boat. Of those on board the other twenty-eight boats, some were killed, some drowned, and the rest brought back prisoners.

The surviving boat, having fifty of the fugitives on board, proceeded down the river, followed by the rebels, who kept up an incessant fire from both banks. At the distance of six miles the boat grounded; its passengers remained passive until night, when the darkness enabled them to shove her off. They pursued their way without interruption, till the boat again grounded at Mussapgurh, eight miles lower down. Here again the rebels attacked the boat, killing many of the passengers; but the assailants were driven off, and retired to Cawnpore. The Nana then immediately despatched two complete regiments in pursuit. At night a violent storm fortunately freed the boat from the sandbank; but, from ignorance of the channel, the boat again grounded further down. When daylight came it showed the unhappy fugitives that their remorseless enemies had followed them up, and were on the bank. They had now reached Sooragpoor, thirty miles from Cawnpore.

As it was found impracticable to move the boat, a party of fourteen landed to drive back their assailants, which they did most effectually; but proceeding too far inland, they were surrounded, and on making their way back to the river, lost all sight of the boat; they accordingly followed the bank for about a mile, when being hotly pressed, they were forced to take refuge and breathing time in a small temple.

At the door of the temple one of the party was killed; the remaining thirteen, after attempting a parley in vain, had recourse to their firelocks, and several of the enemy were killed, or put *hors de combat*. The rebels, fearing even to attack this

small band of Englishmen, brought a gun to bear
on the temple; but finding that it made no impression,
they had recourse to heaping up firewood before
the doorway. Unfortunately, the temple was round,
so that the party within could not prevent their
pushing the wood round to the front. The fire,
however, did not have the desired effect; some
handfuls of powder were therefore thrown on it,
the smoke of which nearly suffocated the fugitives,
who determined to sally and take to the river. On
their charging out of the temple, the enemy fled
in all directions; six or seven of the party (who it
was supposed could not swim) ran into the crowd
and sold their lives as dearly as they could; the
remaining seven threw themselves into the Ganges.
Two of these were shot ere long; a third, resting
himself by swimming on his back, unwittingly
approached too near the bank and was cut up; and
the other four swam six miles down the river, three
of them being wounded. At last, the leader was
hailed by two or three sepoys belonging to a friendly
rajah; who eventually proved to be Maharajah Dig
Bejah Sing, Raja of Raiswarra in Oude.

Exhausted by a three days' fast, and fancying
from their not having been pursued for the last half
mile of the flight that they were safe, the fugi-

tives at once went to the Rajah, who protected and fed them from the 29th of June to the 28th of July. He ultimately provided for their escort to the camp, by a detachment of Europeans proceeding from Allahabad to Cawnpore to join the force under the command of Brigadier-General Havelock.

Of those who were unfortunately captured from the boats, many were killed at once; others, the wives and children of the European officers and soldiers, were placed as prisoners in a house in the cantonments of Cawnpore. Some of these were released from their sufferings by death; others, reserved for a more horrible fate, were killed in batches, as the news of each succeeding victory of the Allahabad avenging column reached Cawnpore.

When General Havelock's force reached Cawnpore, his victory that morning had sealed the fate of the last survivors. On the British force going into cantonments, the marks of butchery and bloodshed were still fresh: the floor of the house in which the prisoners had been confined was foul with clotted blood and tangled masses of hair; and the well close by was filled with mangled corpses. Sadly

[8]   P

and sorrowfully fell the reflection on every heart that they had arrived, alas! too late.

Only four of the victims escaped to tell the tale of the mutiny at Cawnpore.

CROSS ERECTED OVER THE WELL AT CAWNPORE.

London: Printed by SMITH, ELDER and Co., Little Green Arbour Court.

NEW WORKS ON INDIAN AFFAIRS.

1.

THE CHAPLAIN'S NARRATIVE OF THE SIEGE OF DELHI. By the Rev. J. E. W. Rotton. Chaplain to the Forces. Post 8vo. With a Plan of the City and Siege Works. Price 10s. 6d., cloth.

" A simple and touching statement which bears the impress of truth in every word."—*Athenæum*.

" A plain unvarnished record of what came under a field chaplain's daily observation. Our author is a sincere, hard-working, and generous-minded man-"—*Leader*.

" An earnest record by a Christian minister of some of the most touching scenes that can come under observation."—*Literary Gazette*.

" The Chaplain's Narrative is remarkable for its pictures of men in a moral and religious aspect during the progress of a harassing siege, when suddenly stricken down by the enemy or disease."—*Spectator*.

2.

THE CRISIS IN THE PUNJAB, from the 10th of May until the Fall of Delhi. By Frederick Cooper, Esq., C.S., Umritsur. Post 8vo. Price 7s. 6d., cloth.

3.

EIGHT MONTHS' CAMPAIGN AGAINST THE BENGAL SEPOYS, DURING THE MUTINY, 1857. By George Bourchier, Captain Bengal Horse Artillery. With Plans. Post 8vo. Price 7s. 6d. cloth.

4.

PERSONAL ADVENTURES DURING THE INDIAN REBELLION IN ROHILCUND, FUTTEHGHUR AND OUDE. By W. Edwards, Esq., B.C.S., Judge of Benares, and late Magistrate and Collector of Budaon, in Rohilcund. Post 8vo. Price 6s. cloth.

5.

THE PARSEES ; their History, Religion, Manners, and Customs. By Dosabhoy Framjee. Post 8vo. [*Just ready*.

6.

THE DEFENCE OF LUCKNOW: A Diary recording the Daily Events of the Siege from 31st May to 25th September, 1857. By Captain Thomas F. Wilson, 13th Bengal N.I., Assistant-Adjutant-General. 6th Thousand. Small post 8vo, price 2s. 6d., with Plan of Residency.

7.

LIFE AND CORRESPONDENCE OF LORD METCALFE. By John William Kaye. New and Cheap Edition, in 2 vols., small post 8vo, with portrait. Price 12s. cloth.

7.
CHRISTIANITY IN INDIA. By JOHN WILLIAM KAYE, Author of "Life of Lord Metcalfe," &c., 8vo. [*In the press.*

8.
NARRATIVE OF THE MISSION FROM THE GOVERNOR-GENERAL OF INDIA TO THE COURT OF AVA, in 1855. With Notices of the Country, Government, and People. By Captain HENRY YULE, Bengal Engineers. Imperial 8vo, with 24 Plates (12 coloured) 50 Woodcuts, and 4 Maps. Elegantly bound in cloth, with gilt edges. Price 2*l.* 12*s.* 6*d.*

9.
INDIAN SCENES AND CHARACTERS, Sketched from Life. By Prince ALEXIS SOLTYKOFF. Sixteen Plates in Tinted Lithography, with Descriptions. Colombier Folio.
[*Nearly ready.*

10
TRAITS AND STORIES OF ANGLO-INDIAN LIFE. By Lieutenant-Colonel ADDISON. With Eight Illustrations. Small post 8vo. Price 5*s.* cloth.

11.
SUGGESTIONS TOWARDS THE FUTURE GOVERNMENT OF INDIA. By HARRIET MARTINEAU. Second Edition, Demy 8vo. Price 5*s.*, cloth.

12.
BRITISH RULE IN INDIA. By HARRIET MARTINEAU. Second Edition. Demy 8vo. Price 5*s.*, cloth.

13.
VIEWS AND OPINIONS OF BRIGADIER-GENERAL JACOB, C.B. Collected and Edited by Captain LEWIS PELLY, late Political Secretary Persian Expeditionary Force. Demy 8vo. Price 12*s.*, cloth.

14.
THE COMMERCE OF INDIA WITH EUROPE. By B. A. IRVING, Esq., Author of "The Theory and Practice of Caste." Post 8vo. Price 7*s.* 6*d.*, cloth.

15.
TIGER SHOOTING IN INDIA. By Lieutenant WILLIAM RICE, 25th Bombay N.I. Super Royal 8vo. With Twelve Plates in Chromo-lithography. 21*s.*, cloth.

LONDON: SMITH, ELDER AND CO., 65, CORNHILL.

65, *Cornhill, London, July*, 1858.

NEW AND STANDARD WORKS

PUBLISHED BY

SMITH, ELDER & Co.

NEW WORKS.

Gunnery in 1858: *being a Treatise on Rifles, Cannon, and Sporting Arms.* By WILLIAM GREENER, Author of "The Gun."
Demy 8vo, with Illustrations, price 14s., *cloth.* (*Nearly Ready.*)

Personal Adventures during the Indian Rebellion, in Rohilcund, Futteghur, and Oude. By W. EDWARDS, Esq., B.C.S.
Post 8vo, price 6s. *cloth.* (*Now Ready.*)

The Crisis in the Punjab. By FREDERICK H. COOPER, Esq., C.S., Umritsir.
Post 8vo, with Map, price 7s. 6d. *cloth.* (*Now ready.*)

Eight Months' Campaign against the Bengal Sepoys, during the Mutiny, 1857. By Colonel GEORGE BOURCHIER, C.B., Bengal Horse Artillery.
With Plans. Post 8vo, price 7s. 6d. *cloth.* (*Now Ready.*)

The Parsees: their History, Religion, Manners. and Customs. By DOSABHOY FRAMJEE.
Post 8vo. (*Just Ready.*)

Homely Ballads for the Working Man's Fireside. By MARY SEWELL.
Post 8vo, cloth, One Shilling.

Indian Scenes and Characters, Sketched from Life. By Prince ALEXIS SOLTYKOFF.
Sixteen Plates in Tinted Lithography, with Descriptions. Colombier Folio.
(*Nearly Ready.*)

Christianity in India. By JOHN WILLIAM KAYE, Author of "Life of Lord Metcalfe," &c.
8vo. (*In the Press.*)

Lectures and Addresses on Literary and Social Topics. By the late Rev. FRED. W. ROBERTSON, of Brighton. *Post 8vo.* (*Just Ready.*)

NEW PUBLICATIONS.

The Chaplain's Narrative of the Siege of Delhi. By the Rev. J. E. W. ROTTON, Chaplain to the Delhi Field Force.

Post 8vo, with a Plan of the City and Siege Works.

"A simple and touching statement, which bears the impress of truth in every word."—*Athenæum.*

"An earnest record by a Christian minister of some of the most touching scenes which can come under observation."—*Literary Gazette.*

The Defence of Lucknow : A STAFF-OFFICER'S DIARY. By Capt. THOS. F. WILSON, 13th Bengal N. I., Assistant-Adjutant-General.

Sixth Thousand. With Plan of the Residency. Small post 8vo., price 2s. 6d.

"This diary is intrinsically valuable."—*Leader.*

"The 'Staff Officer' supplies exact military information with distinctness."—*Globe.*

"The story of the glorious garrison of Lucknow is told in this volume with all its thrilling and painful details."—*Nonconformist.*

"It has a special interest."—*Examiner.*

Life and Correspondence of Lord Metcalfe. By JOHN WILLIAM KAYE.

New and Cheap Edition, in 2 Vols., Small Post 8vo, with Portrait, price 12s. cloth.

"One of the most valuable biographies of the present day."—*Economist.*

"An edition revised with care and judgment."—*Globe.*

"A new and revised edition of the life of one of the greatest and purest men that ever aided in governing in India."—*Critic.*

Narrative of the Mission from the Governor-General of India to the Court of Ava in 1855. With Notices of the Country, Government, and People. By CAPTAIN HENRY YULE, Bengal Engineers.

Imperial 8vo., with 24 Plates (12 coloured), 50 Woodcuts, and 4 Maps. Elegantly bound in cloth, with gilt edges, price 2l. 12s. 6d.

"A stately volume in gorgeous golden covers. Such a book is in our times a rarity. Large, massive, and beautiful in itself, it is illustrated by a sprinkling of elegant wood-cuts, and by a series of admirable tinted lithographs. . . Captain Yule secures at once an eager reception

of his story. We have read it with curiosity and gratification, as a fresh, full, and luminous report upon the condition of one of the most interesting divisions of Asia beyond the Ganges."—*Athenæum.*

The Education of the Human Race. Now first Translated from the German of LESSING.

Fcap. 8vo, antique cloth, price 4s.

*.** This remarkable work is now first published in English.

"An agreeable and flowing translation of one of Lessing's finest Essays."—*National Review.*

The Essay makes quite a gem in its English form."—*Westminster Review.*

"This invaluable Tract."—*Critic.*

Suggestions Towards the Future Government of India. By HARRIET MARTINEAU.

Second Edition. Demy 8vo, price 5s. cloth.

"The genuine, honest utterances of a clear, sound understanding, neither obscured nor enfeebled by party prejudice or personal selfishness."—*Daily News.*

"As the work of an honest able writer, these Suggestions are well worthy of attention, and no doubt they will generally be duly appreciated."—*Observer.*

NEW PUBLICATIONS—*continued.*

Traits and Stories of Anglo-Indian Life.

By Lieut.-Colonel ADDISON.

With Eight Illustrations, price 5s. cloth.

The Autobiography of Lutfullah, a Mohamedan Gentleman, with an Account of his Visit to England.

Edited by E. B. EASTWICK, Esq.

Third Edition, Small Post 8vo. Price 5s. cloth.

" We have read this book with wonder and delight. Memoirs of a live Moslem gentleman are a novelty in our letters. . . . . Lutfullah's story will aid, in its degree, to some sort of understanding of the Indian insurrection."—*Athenæum.*

" Read fifty volumes of travel, and a thousand imitations of the oriental novel, and you will not get the flavour of Eastern life and thought, or the zest of its romance, so perfectly as in Lutfullah's book. It is readable, instructive, and entertaining."—*Leader.*

" As an autobiography the book is very curious. It bears the strongest resemblance to *Gil Blas* of anything we have ever read."—*Spectator.*

" Everyone who is interested in the present state of matters in India should read Lutfullah's own account of himself and his people, as well as their peculiar and general feeling towards the Feringees."—*Globe.*

" A treasure as well as a rarity in literature."—*Eclectic Review.*

The Life and Correspondence of Sir John Malcolm, G.C.B. By JOHN WILLIAM KAYE.

Two Volumes, 8vo. With Portrait. Price 36s. cloth.

" The biography is replete with interest and information, deserving to be perused by the student of Indian history, and sure to recommend itself to the general reader."—*Athenæum.*

" One of the most interesting of the recent biographies of our great Indian statesmen."—*National Review.*

" This book deserves to participate in the popularity which it was the good fortune of Sir John Malcolm to enjoy."—*Edinburgh Review.*

" Mr. Kaye has used his materials well, and has written an interesting narrative, copiously illustrated with valuable documents."—*Examiner.*

British Rule in India. By HARRIET MARTINEAU.

Fifth Thousand. Price 2s. 6d. cloth.

" A good compendium of a great subject."—*National Review.*

" A succinct and comprehensive volume."—*Leader.*

Tiger Shooting in India.

By LIEUTENANT WILLIAM RICE, 25th Bombay N. I.

Super Royal 8vo. With Twelve Plates in Chroma-lithography. 21s. cloth.

" These adventures, told in handsome large print, with spirited chromo-lithographs to illustrate them, make the volume before us as pleasant reading as any record of sporting achievements we have ever taken in hand."—*Athenæum.*

" A remarkably pleasant book of 'adventures during several seasons of ' large game '

hunting in Rajpootana. The twelve chromo-lithographs are very valuable accessories to the narrative ; they have wonderful spirit and freshness."—*Globe.*

" A good volume of wild sport, abounding in adventure, and handsomely illustrated with coloured plates from spirited designs by the author."—*Examiner.*

MR. RUSKIN'S WORKS ON ART.

Notes on the Pictures in the Exhibition of the Royal Academy, &c., for 1858. By JOHN RUSKIN.
Fifth Thousand. 8vo, price One Shilling.

The Political Economy of Art. Price 2s. 6d. cloth.

" A most able, eloquent, and well-timed work. We hail it with satisfaction, thinking it calculated to do much practical good, and we cordially recommend it to our readers."— *Witness.*

" Mr. Ruskin's chief purpose is to treat the artist's power, and the art itself, as items of the world's wealth, and to show how these may be best evolved, produced, accumulated, and distributed."—*Athenæum.*

" We never quit Mr. Ruskin without being the better for what he has told us, and we therefore recommend this little volume, like all his other works, to the perusal of our readers."—*Economist.*

" This book, daring, as it is, glances keenly at principles, of which some are among the articles of ancient codes, while others are evolving slowly to the light."—*Leader.*

The Elements of Drawing.
Second Edition. Crown 8vo. With Illustrations drawn by the Author.
Price 7s. 6d., cloth.

" The rules are clearly and fully laid down; and the earlier exercises always conducive to the end by simple and unembarrassing means. The whole volume is full of liveliness."— *Spectator.*

" We close this book with a feeling that, though nothing supersedes a master, yet that no student of art should launch forth without this work as a compass."—*Athenæum.*

" It will be found not only an invaluable acquisition to the student, but agreeable and instructive reading for any one who wishes to refine his perceptions of natural scenery, and of its worthiest artistic representations."— *Economist.*

" Original as this treatise is, it cannot fail to be at once instructive and suggestive."— *Literary Gazette.*

" The most useful and practical book on the subject which has ever come under our notice."—*Press.*

Modern Painters, Vol. IV. On Mountain Beauty.
Imperial 8vo, with Thirty-five Illustrations engraved on Steel, and 116 Woodcuts, drawn by the Author. Price 2l. 10s. cloth.

" Considered as an illustrated volume, this is the most remarkable which Mr. Ruskin has yet issued. The plates and woodcuts are profuse, and include numerous drawings of mountain form by the author, which prove Mr. Ruskin to be essentially an artist. He is an unique man, both among artists and writers."—*Spectator.*

" The present volume of Mr. Ruskin's elaborate work treats chiefly of mountain scenery, and discusses at length the principles involved in the pleasure we derive from mountains and their pictorial representation. The singular beauty of his style, the hearty sympathy with all forms of natural loveliness, the profusion of his illustrations form irresistible attractions."—*Daily News.*

Modern Painters, Vol. III. Of Many Things.
With Eighteen Illustrations drawn by the Author, and engraved on Steel.
Price 38s. cloth.

" Every one who cares about nature, or poetry, or the story of human development —every one who has a tinge of literature or philosophy, will find something that is for him in this volume."—*Westminster Review.*

" Mr. Ruskin is in possession of a clear and penetrating mind; he is undeniably practical in his fundamental ideas; full of the deepest reverence for all that appears to him beautiful and holy. His style is, as usual, clear, bold,

racy. Mr. Ruskin is one of the first writers of the day."—*Economist.*

" The present volume, viewed as a literary achievement, is the highest and most striking evidence of the author's abilities that has yet been published."—*Leader.*

" All, it is to be hoped, will read the book for themselves. They will find it well worth a careful perusal."—*Saturday Review.*

WORKS OF MR. RUSKIN—*continued.*

Modern Painters. Vols. I. and II.

Imp. 8vo. Vol. I., 5th *Edit.*, 18s. *cloth.*   *Vol. II.*, 4th *Edit.*, 10s. 6d. *cloth.*

"Mr. Ruskin's work will send the painter more than ever to the study of nature; will train men who have always been delighted spectators of nature, to be also attentive observers. Our critics will learn to admire, and mere admirers will learn how to criticise: thus a public will be educated."—*Blackwood's Magazine.*

"A generous and impassioned review of the works of living painters. A hearty and earnest work, full of deep thought, and developing great and striking truths in art."—*British Quarterly Review.*

"A very extraordinary and delightful book, full of truth and goodness, of power and beauty."—*North British Review.*

The Stones of Venice.

Complete in Three Volumes, Imperial 8vo, with Fifty-three Plates and numerous Woodcuts, drawn by the Author. Price 5l. 15s. 6d., cloth.

EACH VOLUME MAY BE HAD SEPARATELY.

Vol.   I.   THE FOUNDATIONS, *with* 21 *Plates, price* 2l. 2s. 2nd Ed.
Vol. II.   THE SEA STORIES, *with* 20 *Plates, price* 2l. 2s.
Vol. III.   THE FALL,   *with* 12 *Plates, price* 1l. 11s. 6d.

"This book is one which, perhaps, no other man could have written, and one for which the world ought to be and will be thankful. It is in the highest degree eloquent, acute, stimulating to thought, and fertile in suggestion. It will, we are convinced, elevate taste and intellect, raise the tone of moral feeling, kindle benevolence towards men, and increase the love and fear of God."—*Times.*

"The 'Stones of Venice' is the production

of an earnest, religious, progressive, and informed mind. The author of this essay on architecture has condensed into it a poetic apprehension, the fruit of awe of God, and delight in nature; a knowledge, love, and just estimate of art; a holding fast to fact and repudiation of hearsay; an historic breadth, and a fearless challenge of existing social problems, whose union we know not where to find paralleled."—*Spectator.*

The Seven Lamps of Architecture.

Second Edition, with Fourteen Plates drawn by the Author. Imperial 8vo. Price 1l. 1s. cloth.

"By the 'Seven Lamps of Architecture,' we understand Mr. Ruskin to mean the seven fundamental and cardinal laws, the observance of and obedience to which are indispensable to the architect, who would deserve the name. The politician, the moralist, the divine, will find in it ample store of instructive matter, as well as the artist. The author of this work belongs to a class of thinkers of whom we have too few amongst us."—*Examiner.*

"Mr. Ruskin's book bears so unmistakeably the marks of keen and accurate observation, of a true and subtle judgment and refined sense of beauty, joined with so much earnestness, so noble a sense of the purposes and business of art, and such a command of rich and glowing language, that it cannot but tell powerfully in producing a more religious view of the uses of architecture, and a deeper insight into its artistic principles."—*Guardian.*

Lectures on Architecture and Painting.

With Fourteen Cuts, drawn by the Author. Second Edition. Crown 8vo Price 8s. 6d. cloth.

"Mr. Ruskin's lectures—eloquent, graphic, and impassioned—exposing and ridiculing some of the vices of our present system of building, and exciting his hearers by strong motives of duty and pleasure to attend to architecture—are very successful."—*Economist.*

"We conceive it to be impossible that any intelligent persons could listen to the lectures, however they might differ from the judgments asserted, and from the general propositions laid down, without an elevating influence and an aroused enthusiasm."—*Spectator.*

A Portrait of John Ruskin, Esq., Engraved by
F. HOLL, *from a Drawing by* GEORGE RICHMOND.
Prints, One Guinea; India Proofs, Two Guineas.

RECENT WORKS.

Captivity of Russian Princesses in the Caucasus: including a Seven Months' Residence in Shamil's Seraglio, in the Years 1854-5. Translated from the Russian, by H. S. EDWARDS.

With an authentic Portrait of Shamil, a Plan of his House, and a Map.

Post 8vo, price 10s. 6d. cloth.

" A book than which there are few novels more interesting. It is a romance of the Caucasus. The account of life in the house of Shamil is full and very entertaining; and of Shamil himself we see much."—*Examiner.*

" The story is certainly one of the most curious we have read; it contains the best popular notice of the social polity of Shamil and the manners of his people."—*Leader.*

" The narrative is well worth reading."—*Athenæum.*

Esmond. By W. M. THACKERAY, ESQ.

A New Edition in One Volume, Crown 8vo, price 6s. cloth.

" Apart from its special merits " Esmond " must be read just now as an introduction to " The Virginians." It is quite impossible fully to understand and enjoy the latter story without a good knowledge of " Esmond." The two first numbers of " The Virginians " abound with references which can only be properly appreciated by those who have the previous history of the Esmond family fresh in their recollection. The new tale is in the strictest sense the sequel of the old, not only intro-

ducing the same characters, but continuing their history at a later period."—*Leader.*

" Mr. Thackeray has selected for his hero a very noble type of the cavalier softening into the man of the eighteenth century, and for his heroine one of the sweetest women that ever breathed from canvas or from book since Raffaelle painted and Shakspeare wrote. The style is manly, clear, terse, and vigorous, reflecting every mood—pathetic, graphic, or sarcastic—of the writer."—*Spectator.*

The Principles of Agriculture; especially Tropical. By P. LOVELL PHILLIPS, M.D.

Demy 8vo, price 7s. 6d. cloth.

"This volume should be in every farmhouse, and it would pay a landlord to present it to his tenants."—*Critic.*

" This treatise contains nearly all that is known of the science of agriculture."—*Observer.*

Religion in Common Life. By WILLIAM ELLIS.

Post 8vo, price 7s. 6d. cloth.

" A book addressed to young people of the upper ten thousand upon social duties. Mr. Ellis has sound views, and his style is simple and clear."—*Examiner.*

" Lessons in Political Economy for young

people by a skilful hand; a clear knowledge is imparted, and sensible views are worked out to demonstration. We cordially recommend this work to all who are interested in the education of the young."—*Economist.*

Victoria, and the Australian Gold Mines, in 1857; with Notes on the Overland Route. By WILLIAM WESTGARTH.

Post 8vo, with Maps, price 10s. 6d., cloth.

" Mr. Westgarth has produced a reliable and readable book well stocked with information, and pleasantly interspersed with incidents of travel and views of colonial life. It is clear, sensible, and suggestive."—*Athenæum.*

" A lively account of the most wonderful bit of colonial experience that the world's history has furnished."—*Examiner.*

" We think Mr. Westgarth's book much the best which has appeared on Australia since the great crisis in its history."—*Saturday Review.*

" A rational, vigorous, illustrative report upon the progress of the greatest colony in Australia."—*Leader.*

" The volume contains a large amount of statistical and practical information relating to Victoria."—*Spectator.*

" To those who refer to these pages for solid and guiding information, they will prove most valuable."—*Globe.*

" The best book on the subject.—*Critic.*

RECENT WORKS—*continued.*

The Life of Charlotte Brontë.

Author of "JANE EYRE," "SHIRLEY," "VILLETTE," &c.
By MRS. GASKELL, Author of "North and South," &c.

*Third Edition, Revised, Two Volumes, Post 8vo, with a Portrait of Miss Brontë
and a View of Haworth Church and Parsonage. Price 24s. cloth.*

"We regard the record as a monument of courage and endurance, of suffering and triumph. . . . . All the secrets of the literary workmanship of the authoress of 'Jane Eyre' are unfolded in the course of this extraordinary narrative."—*Times.*

"Mrs. Gaskell has produced one of the best biographies of a woman by a woman which we can recall to mind."—*Athenæum.*

"Mrs. Gaskell's 'Life of Charlotte Brontë' has placed her on a level with the best biographers of any country."—*Globe.*

"This work cannot fail to be of the deepest interest: and it has a special interest for female readers."—*Economist.*

"The whole strange and pathetic story of the Brontë family is faithfully told in Mrs. Gaskell's memoir."—*Critic.*

The Sea Officer's Manual; being a Compendium of the Duties of a Commander; First, Second, Third, and Fourth Officer; Officer of the Watch; and Midshipman in the Mercantile Navy. By CAPTAIN A. PARISH, of the East India Merchant Service.

Second Edition, Small Post 8vo, price 5s. cloth.

"A very lucid and compendious manual. We would recommend youths intent upon a seafaring life to study it."—*Athenæum.*

"A little book that ought to be in great request among young seamen."—*Examiner.*

Third Series of Sermons.

By the late REV. FRED. W. ROBERTSON, A.M., Incumbent of Trinity Chapel, Brighton.

Second Edition, Post 8vo, with Portrait, price 9s. cloth.

FIRST SERIES—*Fourth Edition, Post 8vo, price 9s. cloth.*

SECOND SERIES—*Fourth Edition, price 9s. cloth.*

"Very beautiful in feeling and occasionally striking and forcible in conception to a remarkable degree."—*Guardian.*

"Mr. Robertson, of Brighton, is a name familiar to most of us, and honoured by all to whom it is familiar."—*Globe.*

"These sermons are full of thought and beauty. There is not a sermon in the series that does not furnish evidence of originality without extravagance, of discrimination without tediousness, and of piety without cant or conventionalism."—*British Quarterly.*

Antiquities of Kertch, and Researches in the Cimmerian Bosphorus. By DUNCAN McPHERSON, M.D., of the Madras Army, F.R.G.S.,M.A.I., Inspector-General of Hospitals, Turkish Contingent.

Imperial Quarto, with Fourteen Plates and numerous Illustrations, including Eight Coloured Fac-Similes of Relics of Antique Art, price Two Guineas.

"It is a volume which deserves the careful attention of every student of classical antiquity. No one can fail to be pleased with a volume which has so much to attract the eye and to gratify the love of beauty and elegance in

design. . . . . The volume is got up with great care and taste, and forms one of the handsomest works that have recently issued from the English Press."—*Saturday Review.*

RECENT WORKS—*continued.*

Annals of British Legislation, a Classified Summary of Parliamentary Papers. Edited by PROFESSOR LEONE LEVI.

THE TWENTY-THIRD PART IS JUST ISSUED.

"A series that, if it be always managed as it is now by Professor Levi, will last as long as there remains a legislature in Great Britain."—*Examiner.*

"It would not be easy to over-estimate the utility of Professor Levi's serial. It has the

merit of being an excellent idea zealously carried out."—*Athenæum.*

"We cannot imagine a more truly valuable and nationally important work than this. It is impossible to over-estimate its usefulness."—*Civil Service Gazette.*

Life and Sermons of Tauler.
Translated by MISS SUSANNA WINKWORTH. With a Preface by the REV. CHARLES KINGSLEY.
Small 4to, Printed on Tinted Paper, and bound in antique style, with red edges, suitable for a Present. Price 15s.

A Visit to Salt Lake; being a Journey across the Plains to the Mormon Settlements at Utah. By WILLIAM CHANDLESS.
Post 8vo, with a Map, price 9s. cloth.

The Political Life of Sir Robert Peel.
By THOMAS DOUBLEDAY.
Two Volumes, 8vo, price 18s. cloth.

The European Revolutions of 1848.
By EDWARD CAYLEY.
Crown 8vo, price 6s. cloth.

Signs of the Times; or, The Dangers to Religious Liberty in the Present Day. By the CHEVALIER BUNSEN. Translated by Miss SUSANNA WINKWORTH.
One Volume, 8vo, price 16s. cloth.

Stories and Sketches. By JAMES PAYN.
Post 8vo, price 8s. 6d. cloth.

Stoney's Residence in Tasmania.
Demy 8vo, with Plates, Cuts, and a Map, price 14s. cloth.

The Court of Henry VIII.: being a Selection of the Despatches of SEBASTIAN GIUSTINIAN, *Venetian Ambassador,* 1515-1519. Translated by RAWDON BROWN.
Two Vols., crown 8vo, price 21s. cloth.

Sight-seeing in Germany and the Tyrol, in the Autumn of 1855. By SIR JOHN FORBES, Author of "A Physician's Holiday," &c.
Post 8vo, with Map and View, price 10s. 6d. cloth.

RECENT WORKS—*continued.*

Undine. From the German of " De la Motte Fouqué."
Price One Shilling.

Conolly on the Treatment of the Insane.
Demy 8vo, price 14s. cloth.

Hopkins's Handbook of Average.
8vo, price 12s. 6d. cloth.

Morice's Hand-Book of British Maritime Law.
8vo, price 5s., cloth.

Adams's History and Topography of the Isle of Wight.
Quarto, 25 Steel Plates, cloth, gilt edges, price 2l. 2s.

Waring's Manual of Therapeutics.
Fcap. 8vo, price 12s. 6d. cloth.

Vogel on Disorders of the Blood.
Translated by CHUNDER COOMAR DEY.
8vo, price 7s. 6d. cloth.

Duncan's Campaign with the Turks in Asia.
Two Vols., post 8vo, price 21s. cloth.

Ross's Account of Red River Settlement.
One Volume, post 8vo, price 10s. 6d. cloth.

Ross's Fur Hunters of the Far West.
Two Volumes, post 8vo. With Map and Plate. 21s. cloth.

Russo-Turkish Campaigns of 1828-9.
By COLONEL CHESNEY, R.A., D.C.L., F.R.S.
Third Edition. Post 8vo, with Maps, price 12s. cloth.

Thomson's Military Forces and Institutions of Great Britain.
8vo, price 15s. cloth.

The Militiaman at Home and Abroad; being the History of a Militia Regiment.
With Two Etchings, by JOHN LEECH. Post 8vo, price 9s. cloth.

Levi's Manual of the Mercantile Law of Great Britain and Ireland.
8vo, price 12s. cloth.

Thomson's Laws of War Affecting Commerce and Shipping.
Second Edition, greatly enlarged. 8vo, price 4s. 6d. boards.

WORKS ON INDIA AND THE EAST.

The Commerce of India with Europe, and its Political Effects. By B. A. IRVING, Esq., Author of "The Theory and Practice of Caste."
Post 8vo, price 7s. 6d. cloth.

Views and Opinions of Brigadier-General Jacob, C.B. Collected and Edited by Captain LEWIS PELLY, Late Political Secretary Persian Expeditionary Force. *Demy 8vo, price 12s. cloth.*

Papers of the late Lord Metcalfe. Selected and Edited by J. W. KAYE.
Demy 8vo, price 16s. cloth.

The Life of Mahomet and History of Islam to the Era of the Hegira. By WILLIAM MUIR, Esq., Bengal Civil Service.
Two Volumes 8vo, price 32s. cloth.

Tracts on the Native Army of India. By Brigadier-General JACOB, C.B.
8vo, price 2s. 6d.

Rifle Practice. By Brigadier-General JACOB, C.B.
Fourth Edition, 8vo, price 2s.

The English in Western India; being the Early History of the Factory at Surat, of Bombay. By PHILIP ANDERSON, A.M.
Second Edition, 8vo, price 14s. cloth.

Life in Ancient India. By MRS. SPEIR.
With Sixty Illustrations by G. SCHARF. 8vo, price 15s., elegantly bound in cloth, gilt edges.

The Cauvery, Kistnah, and Godavery : being a Report on the Works constructed on those Rivers, for the Irrigation of Provinces in the Presidency of Madras. By R. BAIRD SMITH, F.G.S., Lt.-Col. Bengal Engineers, &c., &c.
In demy 8vo, with 19 Plans, price 28s. cloth.

The Bhilsa Topes ; or, Buddhist Monuments of Central India. By MAJOR CUNNINGHAM.
One Volume, 8vo, with Thirty-three Plates, price 30s. cloth.

The Chinese and their Rebellions.
By THOMAS TAYLOR MEADOWS.
One Thick Volume, 8vo, with Maps, price 18s. cloth.

WORKS ON INDIA AND THE EAST—*continued.*

On the Culture and Commerce of Cotton in India. By Dr. FORBES ROYLE. 8vo, *price* 18s. *cloth.*

Review of the Measures adopted in India for the Improved Culture of Cotton. By Dr. FORBES ROYLE. 8vo, 2s. 6d. *cloth.*

The Fibrous Plants of India fitted for Cordage, Clothing, and Paper. By Dr. FORBES ROYLE. 8vo, *price* 12s. *cloth.*

The Productive Resources of India. By Dr. FORBES ROYLE. Super Royal 8vo, price 14s. cloth.

A Sketch of Assam; with some Account of the Hill Tribes. Coloured Plates, 8vo, price 14s. cloth.

Butler's Travels and Adventures in Assam. One Volume 8vo, with Plates, price 12s. cloth.

Dr. Wilson on Infanticide in Western India. Demy 8vo, price 12s.

Rev. James Coley's Journal of the Sutlej Campaign. Fcap. 8vo, price 4s. cloth.

Crawfurd's Grammar and Dictionary of the Malay Language. 2 vols. 8vo, price 36s. cloth.

Roberts's Indian Exchange Tables. 8vo. Second Edition, enlarged, price 10s. 6d. cloth.

Waring on Abscess in the Liver. 8vo, price 3s. 6d.

Laurie's Second Burmese War—Rangoon. Post 8vo, with Plates, price 10s. 6d. cloth.

Laurie's Pegu. Post 8vo, price 14s. cloth.

Boyd's Turkish Interpreter: a Grammar of the Turkish Language. 8vo, price 12s.

Bridgnell's Indian Commercial Tables. Royal 8vo, price 21s., half-bound.

The Bombay Quarterly Review. Nos. 1 to 9 at 5s. 10 and 12, price 6s. each.

Baillie's Land Tax of India. According to the Moohummudan Law. 8vo, price 6s. cloth.

Baillie's Moohummudan Law of Sale. 8vo, price 14s. cloth.

Irving's Theory and Practice of Caste. 8vo, price 5s. cloth.

Gingell's Ceremonial Usages of the Chinese. Imperial 8vo, price 9s. cloth.

NEW CHEAP SERIES OF POPULAR WORKS.

In Small Post 8vo, with large Type, on good Paper, and neat cloth binding.

Lectures on the English Humourists of the 18th Century. By W. M. THACKERAY, Author of "Vanity Fair," "The Virginians," &c. *Price 2s. 6d. cloth.*

British Rule in India. BY HARRIET MARTINEAU. *Price 2s. 6d., cloth.*

The Political Economy of Art. By JOHN RUSKIN, M.A. *Price 2s. 6d. cloth.*

TO BE FOLLOWED BY

The Town; its Memorable Characters and Events. By LEIGH HUNT.
With 45 Cuts.

AND OTHER STANDARD WORKS.

CHEAP SERIES OF POPULAR FICTIONS.

Well printed, in large type, on good paper, and strongly bound in cloth.

Jane Eyre. By CURRER BELL. *Price 2s. 6d. cloth.*

"'Jane Eyre' is a remarkable production. Freshness and originality, truth and passion, singular felicity in the description of natural scenery, and in the analysation of human thought, enable this tale to stand boldly out from the mass, and to assume its own place in the bright field of romantic literature."—*Times.*

Shirley. By CURRER BELL. *Price 2s. 6d. cloth.*

"The peculiar power which was so greatly admired in 'Jane Eyre' is not absent from this book. It possesses deep interest, and an irresistible grasp of reality. There are scenes which, for strength and delicacy of emotion, are not transcended in the range of English fiction."—*Examiner.*

Villette. By CURRER BELL. *Price 2s. 6d. cloth.*

"This novel amply sustains the fame of the author of 'Jane Eyre' and 'Shirley' as an original and powerful writer."—*Examiner.*

Wuthering Heights and Agnes Grey. By ELLIS and ACTON BELL. With Memoir by Currer Bell. *Price 2s. 6d. cloth.*

A Lost Love. By ASHFORD OWEN. *Price 2s. cloth.*
(*Now Ready.*)

TO BE FOLLOWED BY

Deerbrook. By HARRIET MARTINEAU.

School for Fathers. By TALBOT GWYNNE.

Paul Ferroll. Fourth Edition.

NEW NOVELS.

(TO BE HAD AT ALL LIBRARIES).

Maud Skillicorne's Penance. By MARY CATHERINE JACKSON, Author of "The Story of My Wardship." 2 vols.

"The style is natural, and displays considerable dramatic power."—*Critic.*

The Cruelest Wrong of All. By the Author of "Margaret; or, Prejudice at Home." 1 vol.

"It has the first requisite of a work of fiction—it is amusing."—*Globe.*

The Moors and the Fens. By F. G. TRAFFORD. 3 vols.

"The plot is unhackneyed, and the composition is particularly good."—*Critic.*
"The plot is natural, and skilfully worked out; many of the scenes are described with great power, and the characters look like portraits from life."—*Ladies' Newspaper.*

Gaston Bligh. By L. S. LAVENU, Author of "Erlesmere." 2 vols.

"'Gaston Bligh' is a good story, admirably told, full of stirring incident, and abounding in clever sketches of character."—*Critic.*
"A charming work of fiction."—*Morning Chronicle.*
"The story is told with great power; the whole book sparkles with *esprit.*"—*Press.*

The Three Chances. By the Author of "The Fair Carew." 3 vols.

"The authoress has a mind that thoroughly appreciates the humorous in life and character."—*Globe.*
"This novel is full of good sense, good thought, and good writing."—*Statesman.*

The White House by the Sea : a Love Story. By M. BETHAM-EDWARDS. 2 vols.

Riverston. By GEORGIANA M. CRAIK. 3 vols.

The Professor. By CURRER BELL. 2 vols.

The Noble Traytour. A Chronicle. 3 vols.

Farina ; a Legend of Cologne. By GEORGE MEREDITH. 1 vol.

Below the Surface: a Story of English Country Life. 3 vols.

The Roua Pass ; or, Englishmen in the Highlands. By ERICK MACKENZIE. 3 vols.

Kathie Brande. By HOLME LEE. 2 vols.

Friends of Bohemia ; or, Phases of London Life. By E. M. WHITTY, Author of "The Governing Classes." 2 vols.

Lucian Playfair. By THOMAS MACKERN. 3 vols.

NOVELS FORTHCOMING.

Sylvan Holt's Daughter. By HOLME LEE, Author of "Kathie Brande," &c. 3 vols.

Lost and Won. By GEORGIANA M. CRAIK, Author of "Riverston." 1 vol.

My Lady. 2 vols.

An Old Debt. By FLORENCE DAWSON. 2 vols.

Mutation. 3 vols.

Old and Young. 1 vol.

NEW BOOKS FOR YOUNG READERS.
By the Author of "Round the Fire," &c.

Old Gingerbread and the School-boys.
With Four Coloured Plates.   (*Nearly Ready.*)

Unica: a Story for Sunday.
With Four Cuts.   (*Nearly Ready.*)

Uncle Jack, the Fault Killer.
With Four Illustrations. Price 3s. cloth.
" An excellent little book of moral improve- | yond the common-place moral tale in design
ment made pleasant to children ; it is far be- | and execution."—*Globe.*

Willie's Birthday ; showing how a Little Boy did what he Liked, and how he Enjoyed it.
With Four Illustrations. Price 2s. 6d., cloth

Willie's Rest: a Sunday Story.
With Four Illustrations. Price 2s. 6d. cloth.
" Graceful little tales, containing some pretty | " Extremely well written story books,
parables, and a good deal of simple feeling."— | amusing and moral, and got up in a very
Economist. | handsome style."—*Morning Herald.*

Round the Fire: Six Stories for Young Readers.
Square 16mo, with Four Illustrations, price 3s. cloth.
" Charmingly written tales for the young." | " Simple and very interesting."—*National*
—*Leader.* | *Review.*
" Six delightful little stories."—*Guardian.* | " True children's stories."—*Athenæum.*

The King of the Golden River ; or, the Black Brothers. By JOHN RUSKIN, M.A.
Third Edition, with 22 Illustrations by RICHARD DOYLE. Price 2s. 6d.
" This little fancy tale is by a master-hand. The story has a charming moral."—*Examiner.*

MISCELLANEOUS.

Elementary Works on Social Economy. Uniform in foolscap 8vo, half-bound.

I.—OUTLINES OF SOCIAL ECONOMY. 1s. 6d.

II.—PROGRESSIVE LESSONS IN SOCIAL SCIENCE.

III.—INTRODUCTION TO THE SOCIAL SCIENCES. 2s.

IV.—OUTLINES OF THE UNDERSTANDING. 2s.

V.—WHAT AM I? WHERE AM I? WHAT OUGHT I TO DO? &c. 1s. sewed.

Swainson's Lectures on New Zealand. Crown 8vo, price 2s. 6d. cloth.

Swainson's Account of Auckland. Post 8vo, with a View, price 6s. cloth.

Playford's Hints for Investing Money. Second Edition, post 8vo, price 2s. 6d. cloth.

Sir John Forbes's Memorandums in Ireland. Two Vols., post 8vo, price 1l. 1s. cloth.

Leigh Hunt's Men, Women, and Books. Two Vols. Price 10s. cloth.

———————— *Table Talk.* 3s. 6d. cloth.

———————— *Wit and Humour.* 5s. cloth.

———————— *Jar of Honey.* 5s. cloth.

Sir John Herschel's Astronomical Observations made at the Cape of Good Hope. 4to, with plates, price 4l. 4s. cloth.

Darwin's Geological Observations on Coral Reefs, Volcanic Islands, and on South America. With maps, plates, and woodcuts, 10s. 6d. cloth.

Levi's Commercial Law of the World. Two Vols., royal 4to, price 6l. cloth.

Juvenile Delinquency. By M. HILL and C. F. CORNWALLIS. Post 8vo, price 6s. cloth.

Doubleday's True Law of Population. Third Edition, 8vo, 10s. cloth.

McCann's Argentine Provinces, &c. Two Vols., post 8vo, with illustrations, price 24s. cloth.

Rowcroft's Tales of the Colonies. Sixth Edit. 6s. cloth.

Goethe's Conversations with Eckermann. Translated by JOHN OXENFORD. Two Vols., post 8vo, 10s. cloth.

Kavanagh's Women of Christianity Exemplary for Piety and Charity. Post 8vo, with Portraits, price 12s., in embossed cloth, gilt edges.

POETRY.

The Six Legends of King Goldenstar. By the late ANNA BRADSTREET. Fcap. 8vo, price 5s.

" The author evinces more than ordinary power, a vivid imagination, guided by a mind of lofty aim."—*Globe.*

England in Time of War. By SYDNEY DOBELL, Author of "Balder," "The Roman," &c. Crown 8vo, 5s. cloth.

" That Mr. Dobell is a poet, ' England in time of War' bears witness in many single lines, and in two or three short poems."—*Athenæum.*

The Cruel Sister, AND OTHER POEMS. Fcap. 8vo, 4s. cl.

" There are traces of power, and the versification displays freedom and skill."—*Guardian.*

Poems of Past Years. By Sir ARTHUR HALLAM ELTON, Bart., M.P. Fcap. 8vo, 3s. cloth.

" A refined, scholarly, and gentlemanly mind is apparent all through this volume."—*Leader.*

Poems. By Mrs. FRANK P. FELLOWS. Fcap. 8vo, 3s. cl.

" There is easy simplicity in the diction, and elegant naturalness in the thought."—*Spectator.*

Lota, AND OTHER POEMS. By DEVON HARRIS. Fcap. 8vo, 4s. cloth.

" Displaying high poetic genius and power."—*Eclectic Review.*

Poetry from Life. By C. M. K. Fcap. 8vo, cl. gilt, 5s.

" Elegant verses. The author has a pleasing fancy and a refined mind."—*Economist.*

Poems. By WALTER R. CASSELS. Fcap. 8vo, price 3s. 6d. cloth.

" Mr. Cassels has deep poetical feeling, and gives promise of real excellence. His poems are written sometimes with a strength of expression by no means common."—*Guardian.*

Garlands of Verse. By THOMAS LEIGH. Fcap. 8vo, price 5s. cloth.

" One of the best things in the ' Garlands of Verse' is an Ode to Toil. There, as elsewhere, there is excellent feeling."—*Examiner.*

Balder. By SYDNEY DOBELL. Crown 8vo, 7s. 6d. cloth.

" The writer has fine qualities; his level of thought is lofty, and his passion for the beautiful has the truth of instinct."—*Athenæum.*

Poems. By WILLIAM BELL SCOTT. Fcap. 8vo, 5s. cl.

" Mr. Scott has poetical feeling, keen observation, deep thought, and command of language."— *Spectator.*

Poems. By MARY MAYNARD. Fcap. 8vo, 4s. cloth.

" We have rarely met with a volume of poems displaying so large an amount of power, blended with so much delicacy of feeling and grace of expression."—*Church of England Quarterly.*

Poems. By CURRER, ELLIS, and ACTON BELL. Fcap. 8vo, 4s. cloth.

Select Odes of Horace. In English Lyrics. By J. T. BLACK. Fcap. 8vo, price 4s. cloth.

" Rendered into English Lyrics with a vigour and heartiness rarely, if ever, surpassed."— *Critic.*

London: Printed by SMITH, ELDER & Co., Little Green Arbour Court.

945863

Made in the USA